A TOWN
THROUGH HISTORY

This book takes us on a journey through the centuries. Barma is an imaginary city typical of the northern Mediterranean region. We trace its development from a walled hilltop settlement in the 4th century BC to a great 20th-century metropolis.

Through the history of the city's architecture and the customs of its people, we can follow the development of our civilization. The word 'civilization' is derived from 'city', and living in a city civilized men and women. It taught them to live and work together as a community.

The book features fourteen large drawings of the developing city, each illustrating a different historical stage. Each drawing is followed by two pages of vivid narrative, and specific detailed illustrations keyed to the text.

INTRODUCTION

Barma is an imaginary city; it has never existed and never will exist.
Our imaginary city could have been located almost anywhere along
the Mediterranean coastal strip between Italy and Spain. In many
ways, however, Barma is very real; its network of streets, the walls
that rose up around it and its fine architecture and monuments are
just like those of existing cities in southern Europe as they evolved
through the centuries.

The cultural heritage of Ancient Rome and Western Europe,
shaped by historical events, has given these southern European cities
a certain similarity. These Mediterranean cities were very fortunate.
The heritage of the Roman Empire brought to them a whole range
of cultural traditions, and introduced the stability and civilization we
know today. Later, wars, famines and the arrival of other peoples
with different religions and traditions added to this solid cultural
base.

The story of Barma summarizes, in words and pictures, the
history of a southern European city, from pre-Roman times to the
late 20th century. We hope that our readers, young and not so
young, may learn much that is relevant to their daily lives.

CONTENTS

Introduction   3
  1. The First Farmers   6
  2. A Roman Camp   10
  3. A Large Roman Town   14
  4. The Arrival of the Barbarians   18
  5. The Age of Feudalism   22
  6. The Medieval City   26
  7. Commercial Expansion   30
  8. The Renaissance City   34
  9. The Fortified City   38
10. Enlightenment and Industry   42
11. The Steam Age   46
12. Suburban Expansion   50
13. The Modern City   54
14. Looking to the Future   58
Glossary   62
Further Reading   62
Index   63

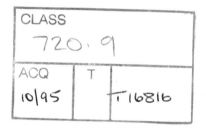
Editor: Rosemary Ashley

English edition first published in 1990 by
Wayland (Publishers) Ltd
61 Western Road, Hove, East Sussex BN3 1JD, England

British Library Cataloguing in Publication Data
Comes, Pilar
A town through history
1. Mediterranean civilisation, history
I. Title II. Hernàndez, Xavier III. Ballonga, Jordi
909' .091822

ISBN 1-85210-991-2

First published in Italy by Editoriale Jaca Book spa, Milano

A TOWN
THROUGH HISTORY

by
XAVIER HERNÀNDEZ and PILAR COMES

illustrated by
JORDI BALLONGA

English translation by
Lucilla Watson

1. THE FIRST FARMERS (4th century BC)

1. THE FIRST FARMERS

(4TH CENTURY BC)

Around the 4th century BC, a small fortified village grew up on a hill near the River Barmo. The people who lived there grew crops and raised animals. They belonged to a group of tribes that dwelt in the river valley. All the tribes in this group were related to one another. The tribes who lived in the Barmo valley were descended from ancient nomadic peoples who had originally moved from Asi settle in the area.

The Barmo valley dwellers were proud of their independe They often fought among themselves or against other gro especially when food was scarce. Then they would fight over g and cattle.

The villagers needed to protect themselves against attack, so built their villages on hilltops, which they could easily defen building ramparts. The steep hillside and defensive walls prote them against surprise attacks. But living in a fortified village c be difficult. Water and firewood had to be carried up the hill and

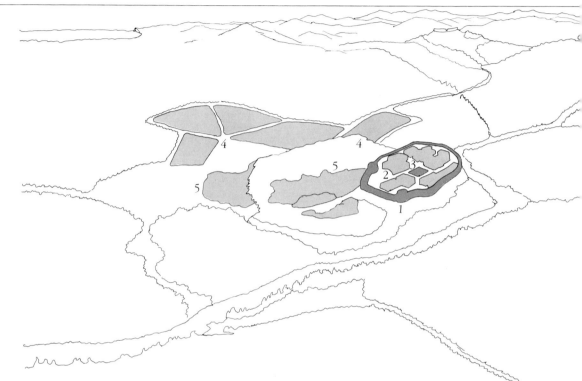

1. Ramparts
The ramparts protected the villagers against attack. Warriors patrolled around the walls, especially during times of war, and they would raise the alarm if necessary. If there was a battle with a neighbouring tribe they fought off the attackers by hurling stones, javelins and arrows. These warriors also carried shields and wore armour.

2. Houses
Houses were built with foundations and lower walls of stone, and upper walls of mud. Rooms were about 3 metres wide so that the wooden beams placed on the walls could support the roof without it collapsing. The roof was made of clay placed on a network of branches. Each house had a hearth and smoke from the fire escaped through an opening in the roof. Some houses were two storeys high. A few smaller houses were used for storing provisions or as sheepfolds.

3. Storage pits
Preserving wheat was very important. Grain was kept in pits dug in the earth and covered with clay. When the pits were completely filled, they were tightly sealed with lids to preserve the grain. The pits were opened again when grain was needed for food or for sowing.*

4. Cultivating fields
Fields planted with crops surrounded the village. When the soil became exhausted, the vil-lagers stopped planting crops there and cleared the trees from new areas. To make a new field, they burnt down the trees, then dug out the roots. After several ploughings, the field was ready for sowing.

5. Olive groves and vineyards
From time to time the villagers met and traded with Greeks who lived lower down the B mo valley. From these peo the villagers learnt about o trees and vines. They grew oli for oil and made wine fr grapes. Olive groves and vi yards grew up around the villa

From ancient times, groups of settlers in lands around the Mediterranean Sea and in most other areas of Southern Europe grew olives and grapes, as well as wheat. For centuries, bread, oil and wine made up the basic diet of people who lived in the lands around the Mediterranean.

le had to be driven inside the walls every night.

Most of the people living in the village spent their days farming land. They cut down the surrounding trees to make open fields ere they could sow their crops. As they did not know about ating crops or allowing fields to lie fallow, the crops they grew n wore out the soil. Then the people had to find other areas to n into fields. They had to look further and further away. After a e, the villagers went off to search for new land where they could ld other villages.

Besides growing crops, these people also owned herds of sheep d goats, and a few oxen which they used for tilling the fields. They also kept horses, on which they rode out to explore surrounding areas.

These people were good builders. They built their villages of stone and mud, and most of the houses were the same shape and size. They stored water in cisterns and dug pits for their grain.

The people knew how to work iron. They used it to make tools and weapons. They also traded with neighbouring villages. They travelled up and down the river valley, so they could reach other areas quite easily.

A PRE-ROMAN HOUSE
1. Stone foundations and lower walls
2. Mud walls
3. Oak or wild olive beams
4. Hearth
5. Loom
6. Mud used as cement between timbers
7. Roof of mud and branches
8. Basket weaving
9. Millstone
10. Storage pits

IRON-WORKING Pieces of iron ore were sandwiched between logs of wood and covered with clay to make an oven. With the help of bellows, the wood burnt at a high temperature; the iron ore melted, separating out the pure iron.

The iron obtained by this method was beaten hard while it was still red hot, to make it hold together. Later, it was beaten or moulded into tools and other implements.

9

2. A ROMAN CAMP (2nd century BC)

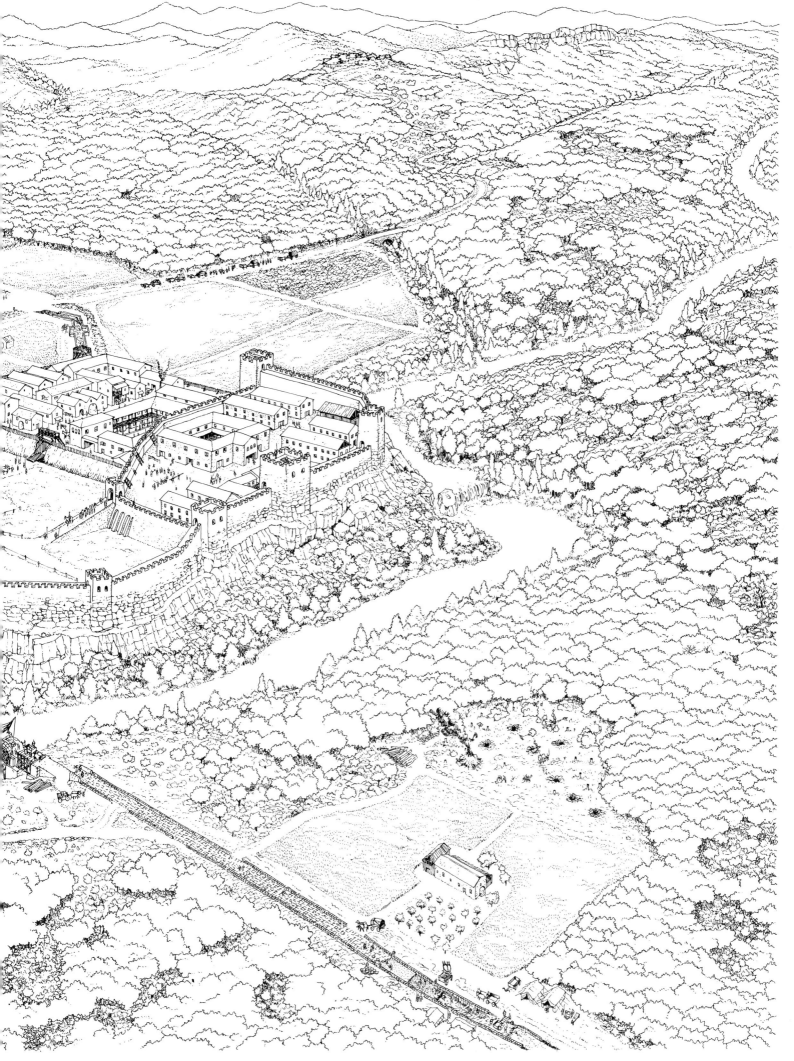

2. A ROMAN CAMP

(2ND CENTURY BC)

In 218 BC, Hannibal's army marched through the Barmo valley. The valley played an important part in the war which was shaking the Mediterranean world from end to end. Rome and Carthage, the two greatest powers of the time, were locked in deadly battle. After a brilliant military compaign, Hannibal had almost reached the gates of Rome. The Romans quickly launched a counter-attack in several directions. They took control of the Barmo valley and brought to heel its inhabitants, who had formed alliances with the Carthagini... Many villages in the valley were destroyed and their inhabita... scattered. The Romans built fortresses at strategic points, to s... troops and supplies passing through on their way to help Hanni...

On a hill where a native village had once stood, the Romans b... a camp. This camp was circled by a strong wooden fence an... defensive ditch. Inside, tents were put up for the troops who v... stationed there to defend the valley.

When the Second Punic War was over (201 BC), the Romans k... their armies in place so that they could control the area and conti... colonizing and making use of the land. They strengthened t...

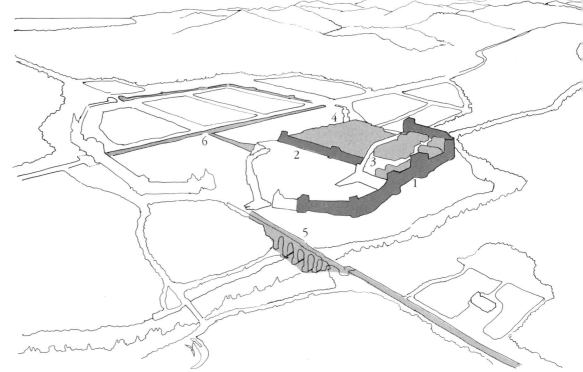

1. Defensive walls
After the period of the Punic Wars, thick walls were built around some of the Roman camps. The bases of these walls were built with enormous boulders. The boulders were topped with cut stones cemented together with a mixture of lime, sand and water.

2. Fences
Roman soldiers quickly built makeshift fortifications by digging ditches and setting up wooden fences.

3. Soldiers' quarters
When the camp became an almost permanent settlement, the tents were replaced by more comfortable huts and lean-tos where the soldiers slept. This was also where they stored weapons and other machinery of war, and where the horses and cattle were stabled.

4. Outlying settlements
Soon, small settlements appeared all around the permanent camp. The families of some of the soldiers lived in the settlements, along with shopkeepers and traders who had arrived in the area. The soldiers came to the settlements when they were off duty. Here they could relax in the taverns and enjoy the warm baths.

5. Roads and bridges
The Romans built firm roads and magnificent bridges, so that they could move their troops about more easily, and also to open up the land to trade and exploitation of natural resources. In this way they established lines of communication throughout their growing empire. All this building also served to display the greatness, the skill and the power of Rome.

6. Planning new towns
New towns were carefu... planned and built in positio... that the Romans thought w... suitable. Town planners trac... the lay-out of the streets, a... solved problems such as ... laying of foundations and ... stallation of drainage system...

BUILDING A BRIDGE
1. Wooden supports are put in place
2. Lime is dried to build the base
3. The pillars are put up
4. Building the arches supported by wooden frames
5. Detail of the pulley system

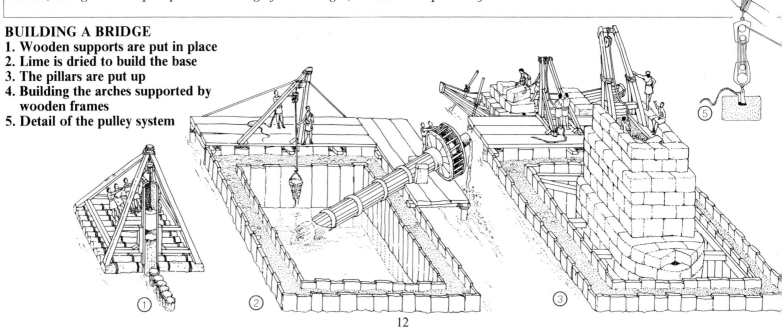

p with thick stone walls and tents were replaced by stone huts. Romans called the camp Barminia, and from it the IXth Legion down all attempts at rebellion by the Barmo valley peoples who been attempting to rebel for many years. By the middle of the century BC, the valley was peaceful and completely under nan control. It had become part of the Roman world. The Barmo ples had begun to speak Latin and to adopt Roman customs and Roman way of life. The camp was starting to look like a small n. In addition to the soldiers and their huts, servants, officials traders were living in settlements nearby.

o help spread the Roman way of life in the land, the Romans decided the establish a colony. They proceeded to build a new large town. This town would be a centre for exploiting the valley and for keeping the area under Roman control.

The soldiers set to work, cutting down the trees around their camp. Surveyors and engineers marked out the edges of the city that was to be built, and planned the layout of the streets. Groups of soldiers and teams of slaves erected a bridge and built wide roads. Now the Romans would not have to march along rough muddy tracks or risk fording dangerous rivers.

ILDING A ROAD

aved surface
lard core
ubble
nfill
mile stone
urveyors using a levelling device

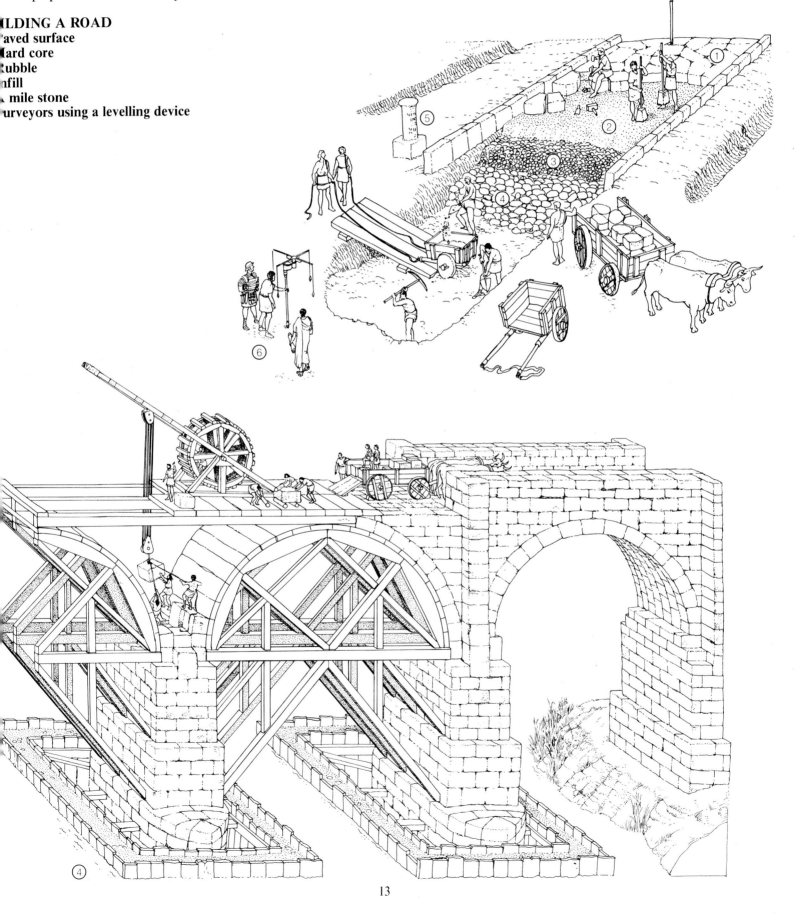

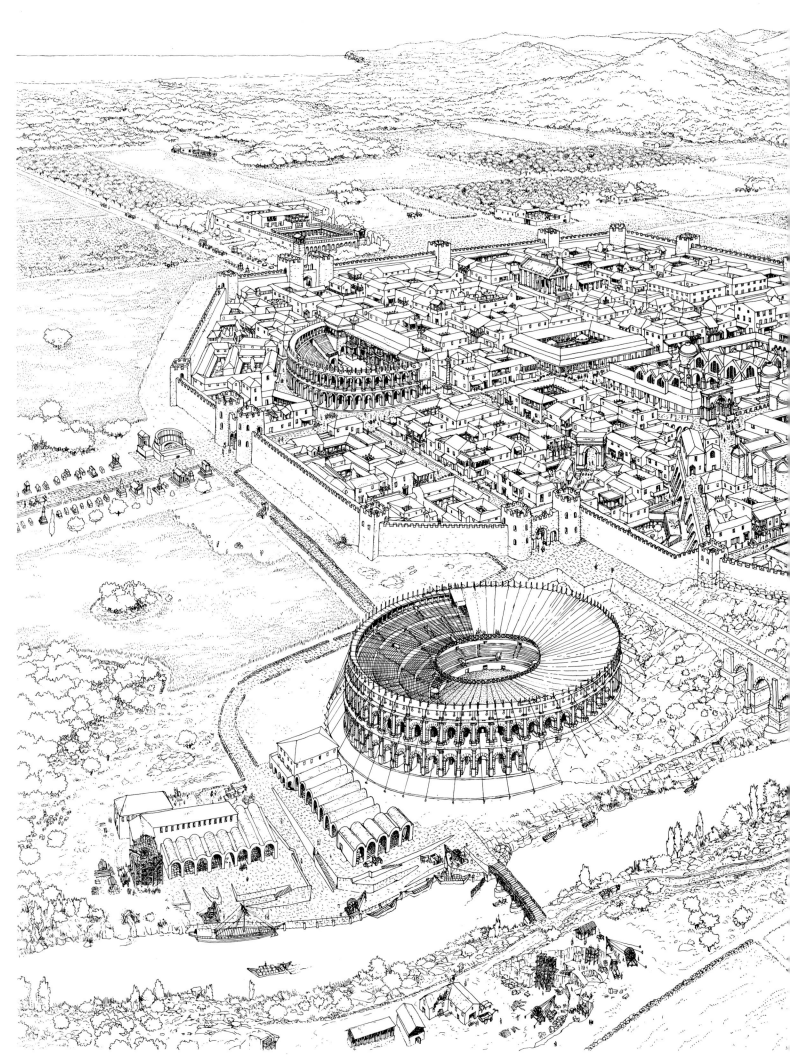

3. A LARGE ROMAN TOWN (2nd century AD)

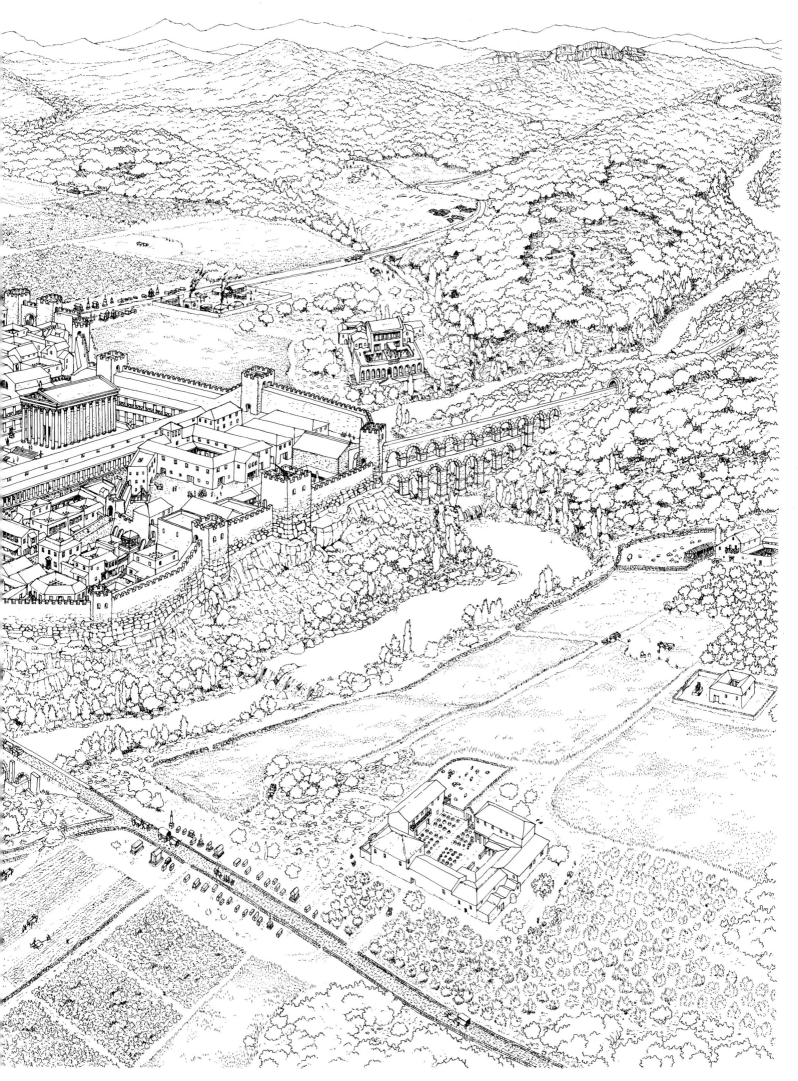

3. A LARGE ROMAN TOWN
(2ND CENTURY AD)

As time went on, the colony of Barminia grew, soon becoming the most prosperous town in the Barmo valley. It was given the name Colony of Julia Augusta Barminia, in honour of some of its protectors. The town reached its greatest splendour at the beginning of the 2nd century, when Trajan was Roman Emperor.

The town centre was completely built up and the outsk stretched down to the foot of the hill on which the Romans had f built their camp. The rock on the steep hillside had been neatly a patiently hacked away to make three terraces, turning the slope i level areas.

There were a number of important squares and public buildi in Barminia. These included the forum, with its temple dedicated the Emperor Augustus, the basilica, the tribunal and the triump arch, baths and a theatre. Outside the walls, an amphitheatre I been built, partly cut into the rock, making the most of the sl of the hillside.

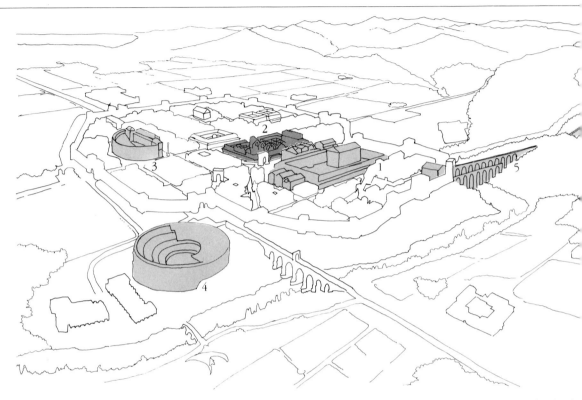

1. The forum
The forum was a large open square lined with porticos. It contained the temple, the tribunal, where military commanders and magistrates who governed the city, gathered together; and the basilica, where judges sat and where trading took place. The forum was also a convenient place to stroll and chat. Its porticos provided shade from the heat of the sun and shelter on rainy days.

2. The baths
Personal hygiene was very important to the Romans. While they washed in the warm water, there was time for a leisurely chat. Some baths were equipped with a gymnasium, massage rooms and libraries. This was a good place to spend a few hours with friends.

3. The theatre
The theatre was semi-circular. Contemporary plays were sometimes performed there, as well as the classics of Greek and Roman drama.

4. The amphitheatre
When games were being held, this was one of the most crowded places. The most frequent events were contests with wild animals and combat between gladiators. An awning sheltered spectators from the sun.

5. The aqueduct
Running water was brought to the town by means of an aqueduct. Water from springs and rivers was channelled off at points above the town. It flowed down the aqueduct and reached the city, where it was stored in a

reservoir located in a high pla From there, water ran to parts of the town through slo ing pipes and small channe Dirty water trickled throu drains leading to the river.

he area on top of the hill was still occupied by soldiers and their
pment. It housed part of the IIIrd Legion, the bodyguard of the
rnor of the province and officials of the Roman Empire. On the
level down were the forum and several administrative centres.
on this level were a market square and many large and
rious houses. On the lower level were public buildings such as
theatre and the baths, and the houses of ordinary people. These
ses were spread over a wide area. Many of them, with several
rs, stood out above the rest. Here also were many shops,
ehouses and workshops, where almost anything could be
ght, sold or made.

A port was built on the river outside the walls. From there, wine,
oil, earthenware pots and jars and goods manufactured in the town
or in outlying areas were shipped down to the Mediterranean.

Coming from the east, a wide road passed over a magnificent
bridge and led into Barminia. It linked up with the west and the
north-to-south roads, each one passing under a main gate. Beside
these roads were the cemeteries.

At this time about 10,000 people lived in Barminia, including citizens, freed slaves, slaves and foreigners. Several villas had been built
on the agricultural estates around the town. The fields had been divi-
ded into rectangular plots of land, producing a rich harvest of crops.

INSULA OR ORDINARY MULTI-STOREY HOUSE

1. Fountain
2. Drains
3. Pipe and channels
   for water
4. Workshop
5. Butcher's shop
6. Tavern
7. Living rooms on
   various floors

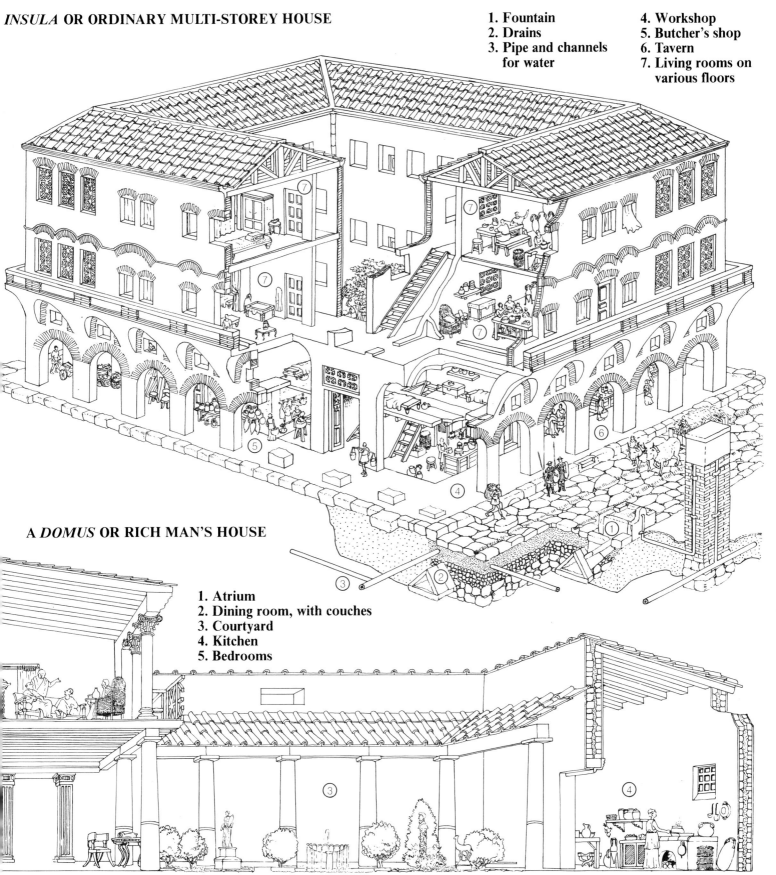

A *DOMUS* OR RICH MAN'S HOUSE

1. Atrium
2. Dining room, with couches
3. Courtyard
4. Kitchen
5. Bedrooms

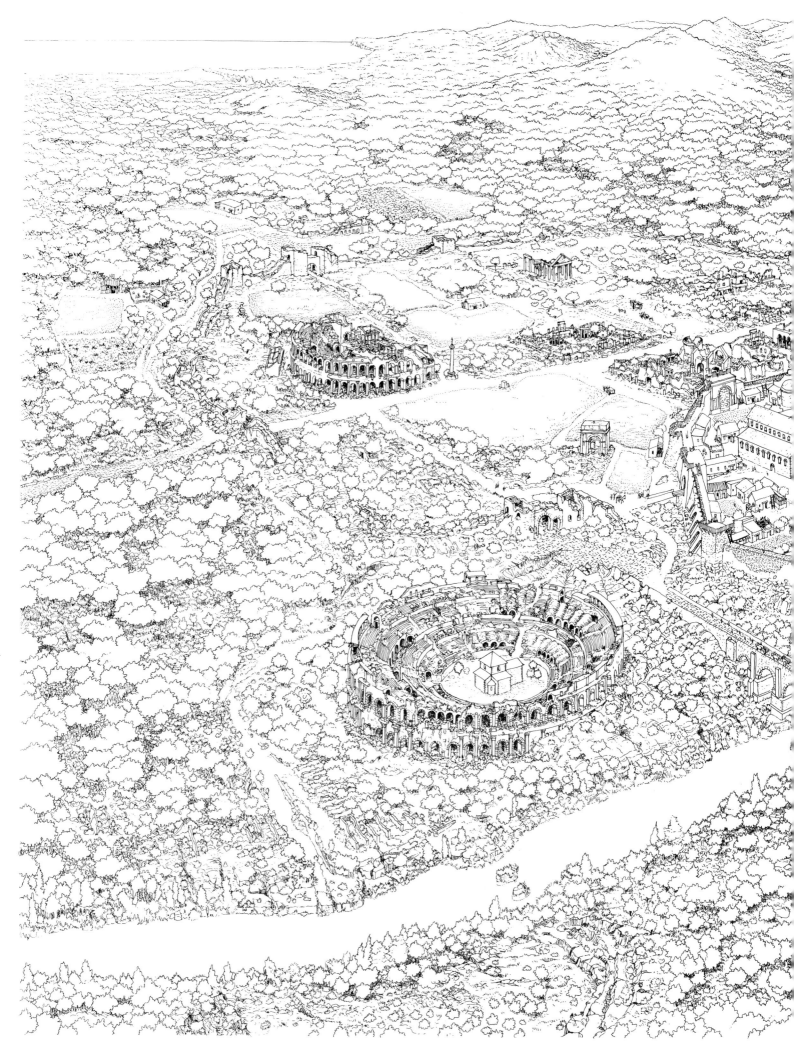

4. THE ARRIVAL OF THE BARBARIANS (6th century)

4. THE ARRIVAL OF THE BARBARIANS
(6TH CENTURY)

Although life in Barminia continued peacefully for many years, the collapse of the Roman Empire was eventually to affect the town. At the end of the 3rd century, Barminia began to be attacked by groups of Barbarians who had broken through the frontiers of the Empire. The town was destroyed. Those who survived the attack rebuilt the ramparts, using stones and rubble from the ruined buildings. Du the 4th century, the Roman Empire went through more cr Roman towns slowly lost their importance as centres of trade, became deserted. Many people, especially the rich, fled to safet the countryside.

Towns were now unsafe to live in and Roman armies coulc longer protect the frontiers of the Empire.

Besides the danger of attack from Barbarians, there were o troubles. An economic and social crisis was tearing the Ron Empire apart. Townspeople and peasants rebelled, causing end civil and class wars.

1. The fortified palace
The Barbarian chiefs built their houses from the remains of earlier buildings. The great Roman building skills were forgotten. These new houses were roughly built, with bulky stone walls and small doors and windows.

2. The basilica and baptistry
Christianity had taken a strong hold from the time of the Emperor Constantine (AD 280-337). It became the official religion of the Roman Empire. Bishops, priests and other church officials became very powerful, soon having as much influence as kings. The basilica was a large building, big enough to hold the Christians who gathered for worship. It was better suited to the new religion than the old temples where statues of the gods had stood. Behind the basilica was the baptistry, where the faithful were christened by immersion in water.

3. New ramparts
As the town's population decreased, so the extent of the walls was re-defined. The town was now centred on areas that were high up or that could be easily defended. New ramparts were built, taking advantage of what walls were still standing or re-using stones from the ruins. Parts that had been built by the Romans were carefully mended and built up to make them even stronger.

4. New shrines
Shrines were put up in various places. During the 6th century in Barminia, a martyrs' shrine was put up in the amphitheatre in honour of Saint Argenio and Saint Eulalia who, it was said, had been sacrificed there in the 3rd century.

5. Ruins of Roman buildings
Most of the Roman public buildings, along with private houses, had been destroyed by fires or battles, or had simply been abandoned. These ruins were turned into convenient quarries for building materials. Some Roman stonework, like the ram-

parts and the bridges, were restored and kept in good order because they were useful. People *now drew their water from ne ly dug wells or the ciste already built.*

AN EARLY CHRISTIAN CHURCH AND BAPTISTRY

Basilicas and their baptistries were the most typical Christian buildings during the final years of the Roman Empire and the time of the Barbarian kingdoms. They were places of worship where religious ceremonies took place, bringing together the Christian community.

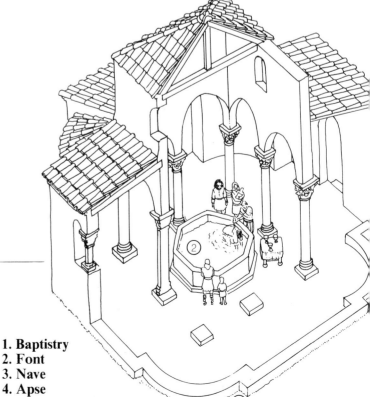

1. Baptistry
2. Font
3. Nave
4. Apse
5. Wooden roof beams

rom the beginning of the 4th century the arrival and spread of ~~i~~stianity, a new religion, improved the situation slightly, but it ~~d~~ not stop the slow disintegration of the Roman Empire.

~~B~~arminia suffered severely. Many of its houses and other ~~buil~~dings stood in ruins, and hovels were built from the rubble. The ~~pop~~ulation was drastically reduced, and by the end of the 4th ~~cent~~ury, fewer than 3,000 people lived in the town. By the middle of ~~the~~ 5th century, Barminia had become part of one of the many ~~Barb~~arian kingdoms into which the Roman Empire had been split. ~~In~~ the 6th century, a Barbarian chief built a fortified palace in ~~Bar~~minia. With his warriors, he governed the whole region of lower

Barmo. The top part of the town was once again fortified. People lived mainly on the middle level, around the basilica that had been built in the 4th century. The lower part of the town had been abandoned and only ruins remained.

Most of the 1,500 inhabitants now living there were of Roman descent, like almost all the other people in the area. They kept to their old customs, and went on speaking their own language. The Barbarian warriors and their families formed a smaller group but they controlled the other inhabitants. They mostly fought wars with the peoples of Eastern Europe, who were trying to take over the Barmo valley.

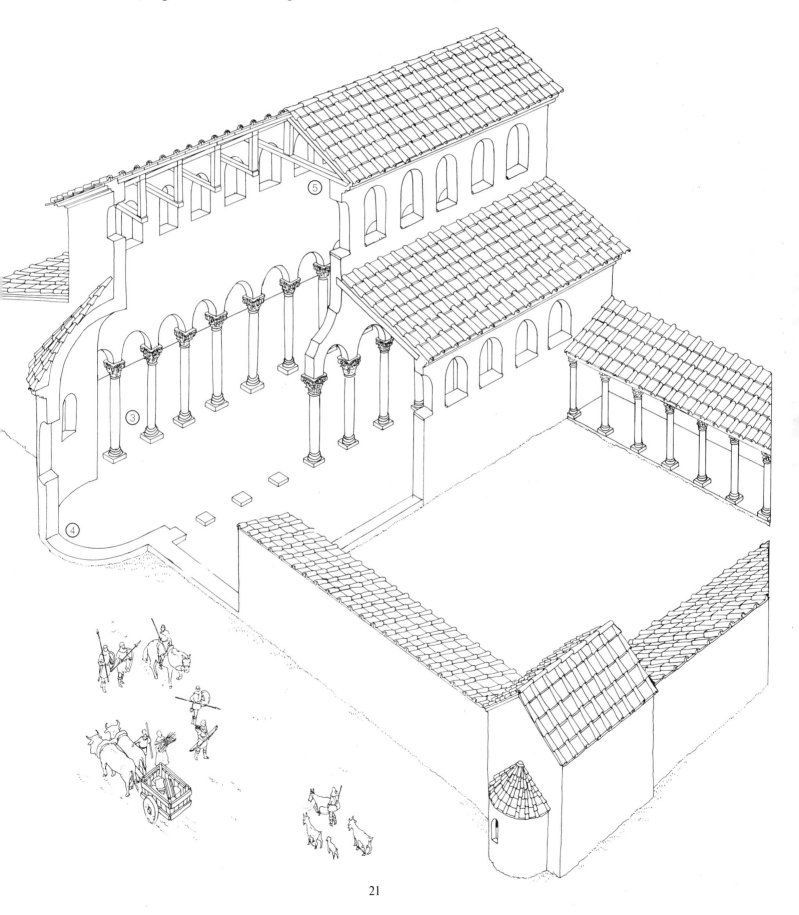

5. THE AGE OF FEUDALISM (late 11th century)

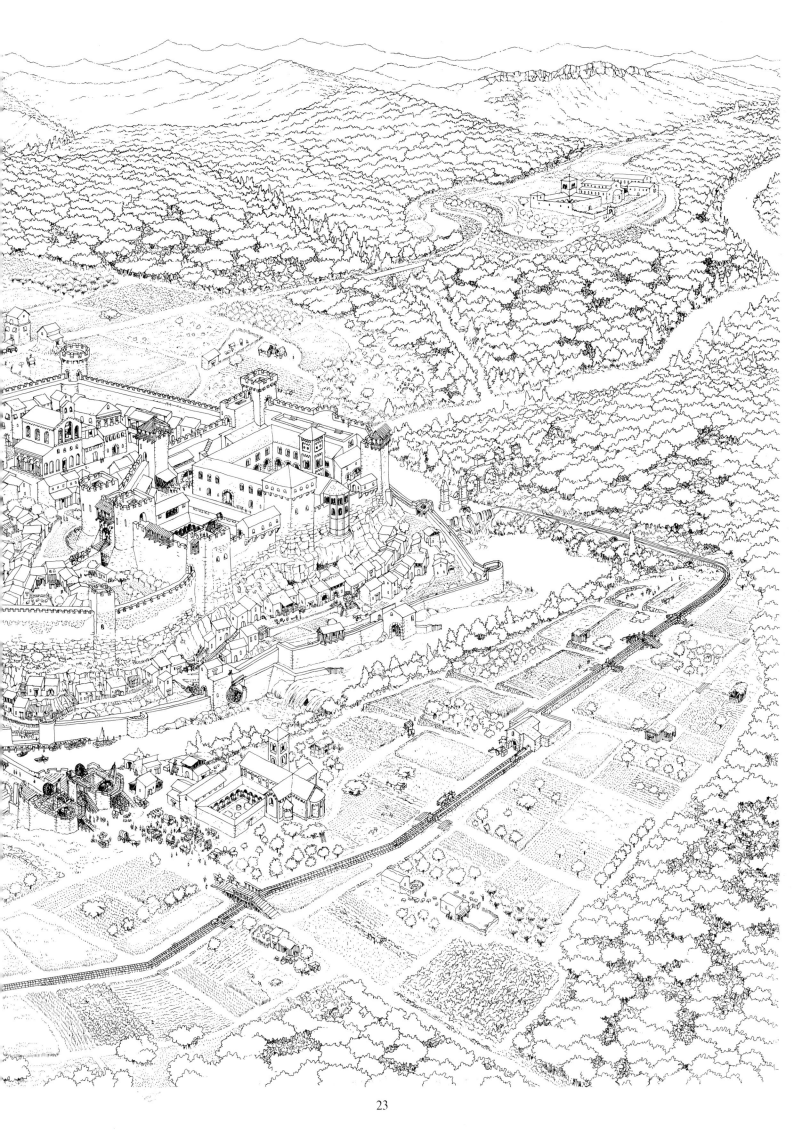

5. THE AGE OF FEUDALISM
(LATE 11TH CENTURY)

At the beginning of the 9th century, Barminia formed par[t] Charlemagne's Frankish Empire. The Franks kept a garrison in [the] town to control the area. As time went by, Charlemagne's em[pire] collapsed and the feudal system took over the whole of Europe[.]

By the end of the 11th century, Barminia, now known as Bar[ma] had become the capital of a growing feudal earldom. The people [who] lived in this earldom were mostly farmers ruled over by knights [and] churchmen. The Earl of Barma built his fortified palace right at [the] top of the town. It housed the officials who looked after his la[nds.]

The people now spoke a new language, which had developed f[rom] Latin. Their customs and way of life had also changed.

For the last few centuries, times had been hard in Barminia. As the wars went on, the town was attacked and destroyed again and again. But people went on living there because of the town's sturdy walls and its strategic location in the area.

1. The earl's palace
The earl's palace was first built in traditional style. During the 11th century it was rebuilt and designed in the Romanesque style. The rooms of the earl's clerks and officials, and the stables, the guardsmen's quarters and the chapel were arranged on either side of a covered courtyard.

2. The cathedral
The cathedral was a very important, central point of medieval cities. It was a large and splendid building, and the most important church in the bishop's diocese. The buildings around the cathedral housed the priests and other church officials, and the offices of the clerks.

3. The monasteries
The monastic way of life was very important during the Middle Ages. Monasteries were usually built outside the city walls and in places where a saint was said to have been martyred. Monasteries were self-sufficient, with their own lands and their own riches. Their libraries were *the universities of the time, where manuscripts and books on science and religion were patiently copied out.*

4. A water mill
During the late Middle Ages, running water was widely used for grinding grain into flour. *Large wheels were turned by the water and, connected by shafts and axles, they moved millstones round to grind the grain.* *Water mills were mainly own[ed] by feudal overlords, who c[ol]lected money from people w[ho] wanted to use them.*

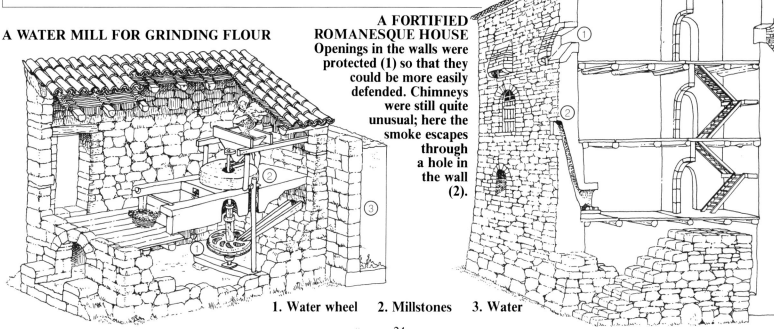

A WATER MILL FOR GRINDING FLOUR

A FORTIFIED ROMANESQUE HOUSE Openings in the walls were protected (1) so that they could be more easily defended. Chimneys were still quite unusual; here the smoke escapes through a hole in the wall (2).

1. Water wheel 2. Millstones 3. Water

The whole town now had about 3,000 inhabitants. At the
[be]ginning of the 11th century, the ancient basilica was knocked
[dow]n and work started on a splendid new Romanesque cathedral.
[The] bishop had also built himself a palace, from which he
[ad]ministered all the churches in the earldom. Apart from orchards,
[veg]etable gardens and a few other open spaces, almost all the city
[cen]tre had now been built up.

[C]raftsmen who worked for the Church or the earl lived in the
[hou]ses, along with a few peasants who worked on the nearby land.
[The]re was also a Jewish quarter, where trade took place and money
[cha]nged hands.

Outside the walls, peasants' houses clustered around new churches.
Monasteries were also built. The monks prayed together, worked the
land and grew crops.

To make it easier to water the land, the earl ordered his men to dig
an irrigation ditch. Water mills were set up on the riverbanks for
grinding the city's grain. A trade network was starting up over the
whole area and Barma was at the centre of it. The town was growing
very fast.

[R]OMANESQUE CHURCH
[N]aves, or aisles
[A]pse
[D]ome
[A]rches built with stone and cement
[T]ransverse arch
[P]illar
[B]uttress
[S]caffolding and frames for building an arch
[S]tone-cutters and carpenters, the most important craftsmen in the
[b]uilding process, working under the orders of the foreman

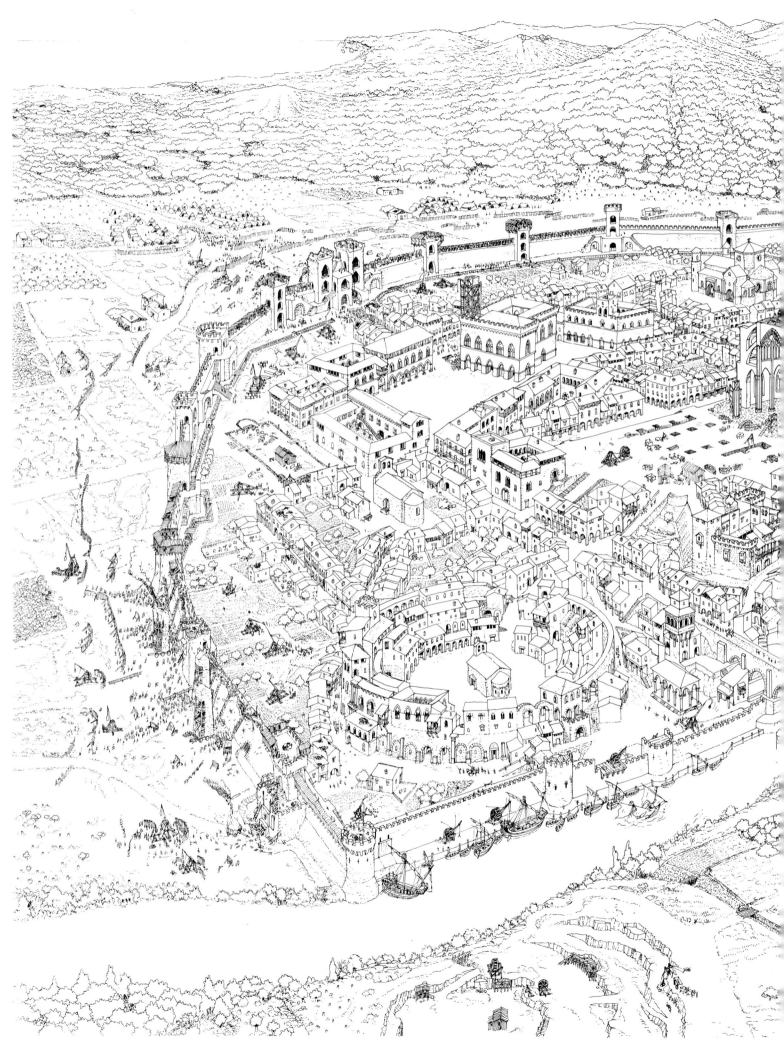

6. THE MEDIEVAL CITY (mid - 13th century)

6. THE MEDIEVAL CITY
(MID - 13TH CENTURY)

Barma grew very fast during the 12th and 13th centuries. The wine and oil produced in the area, along with the woollen cloth woven in the city's workshops and swords and other articles manufactured in the forges, all produced a flourishing trade. The people of Barma exported their products to towns in distant areas. They traded these for other items that were in turn transported to Barma; some were luxuries, others were everyday goods. All this was part of the busy process of buying and selling that went on at various towns in Mediterranean region. By the middle of the 13th century, the had 7,000 inhabitants.

The river port was enlarged and canals were dug so that bo could more easily sail to and from the port.

More and more workshops were needed and new streets w constructed. Because the centre of the city was completely built these streets were built on the outside of the city walls. The encouraged trade and rewarded those of his citizens who sw allegiance to him. The citizens governed themselves throug council which decided how the city should be run.

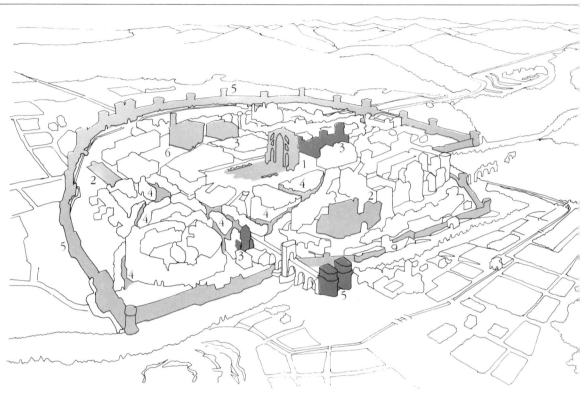

1. The cathedral
Many cathedrals in the Gothic style were built during the 13th and 14th centuries. Sometimes the old Romanesque cathedrals and churches were altered, enlarged or abandoned in favour of the new style now popular in Western Europe. At other times, Romanesque churches were knocked down and replaced by Gothic churches.

2. Convents and monasteries
New kinds of religious buildings—the convents and monasteries for nuns and monks—appeared in the city close to the walls. With their churches, cloisters, gardens and other buildings, they occupied a lot of space.

3. Wealthy residences
Some of the noblemen and rich tradesmen built themselves comfortable palaces, with a central courtyard and many outbuildings. Their towers were almost as tall as the church bell-towers.

4. Craftsmen's streets
Craftsmen working at the same trade often clustered together in the same street or area of the city. That is why so many streets in medieval towns are named after crafts and trades. The craftsmen formed societies called guilds. They held meetings in the house where their guild was based; the papers on which the guild's rules and decisions were written down were also kept there.

5. City walls
As cities grew in size, their walls were expanded. City walls were very important because they provided protection for the inhabitants. At the same time, a careful watch was kept from the city gates on all the merchandise that came in and out of the city.

6. The town hall
The town council, the citize system of self-government, w soon given its own buildir Here, meetings took place, cords and documents were ke and consignments of goods we delivered and services organize As time went on and cities came richer, town halls becar increasingly ornate.

DEFENDING AND BESIEGING CITIES
1. **The main gates of the city were protected by towers and drawbridges.**
2. **The attackers were showered with stones and arrows thrown or shot from the towers and battlements.**
3. **Catapults and other machinery of war were used to attack walls and to defend them.**
4. **Making a fire and setting up a mine to blast a hole in the wall was a tactic used by attackers.**

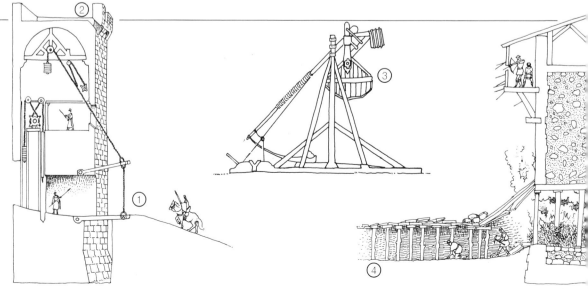

Many busy hamlets and larger groups of houses grew up alongside the roads running into the city. More and more were built until they almost surrounded the city. The council decided to build a new wall that would take in all the city's new houses. Work also started on a new town hall, which would be built opposite a new square. This was to be a symbol of the citizens' new importance.

The old Romanesque cathedral was small and dark. At the beginning of the century, the bishop decided to build a new one. The merchants, the guilds of tradesmen and the noblemen all contributed towards the cost of the work. The new cathedral was built in the Gothic style, and took 112 years to complete.

Inside the city walls, new kinds of religious buildings grew up. These were the monastic buildings for the new orders of nuns and monks who had sworn to live a poor and simple life. A large hospital was also built at this time. It was originally for poor people but as time went by it became the city's general hospital. Barma's university was founded in a group of buildings near the town hall. The university was to become famous for its school of medicine.

Occasional periods of siege and a few religious battles were the only times that the peace of Barma was disturbed. At the end of the 13th century, Jews, and others, thought to be heretics, were persecuted and their houses destroyed.

BUILDING A GOTHIC CATHEDRAL

1. Arch
2. Large window
3. Buttress
4. Gargoyle
5. Flying buttress
6. Pinnacle
7. Winch
8. Nave
9. Carpenters
10. Stonemasons, sculptors and glaziers

7. COMMERCIAL EXPANSION (mid - 15th century)

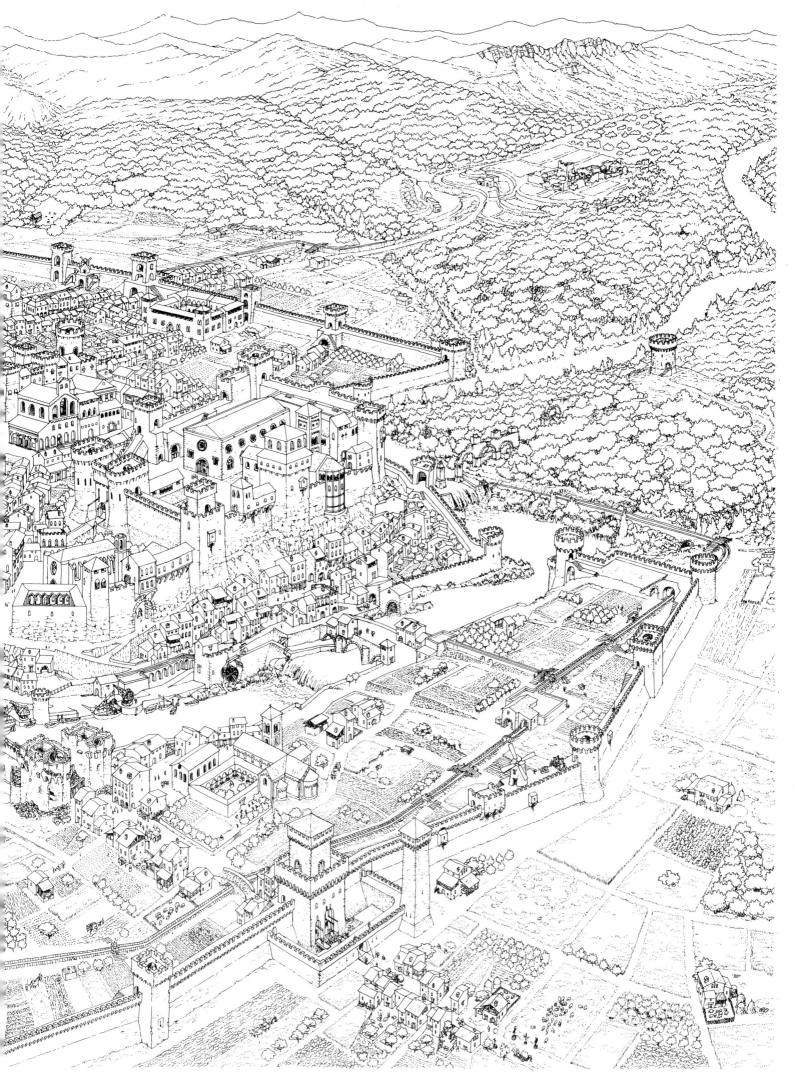

7. COMMERCIAL EXPANSION
(MID - 15TH CENTURY)

In the 14th and early 15th centuries, Barma went on expanding, although at a slower rate. Terrible epidemics of plague and other diseases were sweeping through Western Europe. These, along with bloody revolutions, civil wars and struggles for control of the city, affected population growth.

By the middle of the 15th century, Barma's population was 14, and the city's growth was resumed. Areas inside the walls which been kept for gardens were now built up. The cluster of building the other side of the river had grown and had a wall built aroun. It seemed as if the city would never stop expanding.

Major re-organization took place inside the walls. The town was enlarged and given a new façade. What from now on woul the main square and the city's focal point was opened up oppo. Within the square's arcades countless events, including markets celebrations, would take place. The square was one of the city's o spaces, but there were also smaller squares next to parish churc

1. The main square
This was the nerve centre of the city, just as the forum had been in Roman times. The town hall, pride of the townspeople, overlooked it. Its porticos gave shade in the summer and shelter on rainy days. Markets, games, sporting contests, tournaments and celebrations took place in the wide square.

2. The Town Hall
In the 15th century, the town hall became one of the most important and prominent buildings in the city. The city's prosperity contributed to its imposing appearance. The building had many rooms, including a great meeting hall or council chamber. The high tower housed a clock. As the clock struck the hours, the townspeople could organize their day.

3. The university
Subjects studied in medieval universities were mainly theology, law, the priesthood, philosophy, rhetoric, Greek, Latin and medicine. Universities contained classrooms and special laboratories, as well as living quarters for teachers and students.

4. The merchants' hall
The merchants' hall was a spacious building where merchants displayed their goods, traded, gossiped and haggled over goods and prices.

5. The exchange
As trade and commerce developed in late medieval cities, the first financial institutions, the ancestors of modern banks, appeared. Money changers bankers lent funds, offer securities, received money safe-keeping and handled sorts of financial business.

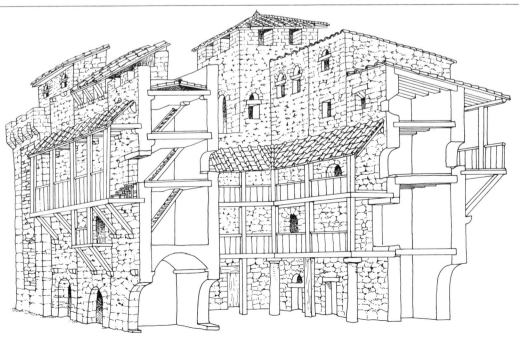

TOWER HOUSES
Some noble families made th homes in tower houses. Dispu and rivalries between grou and families in a town mad safer to live somewhere t could be defended in case quarrels. The tower house v ideal for these conditions cause it was very like a fortif tower. Members of a family a their relatives used to live blocks of tower houses b close together.

were used as graveyards and as places in which to sit and relax. ...monastic buildings were enlarged and altered, some becoming ...large indeed.

...spite of the troubles, trading went on, and, from the profit that ...ought to the town, new palaces were built and existing ones ...roved. In some parts of the city, lack of space meant that houses ...w upwards. The guilds worked hard and the benefits of their ...th could be seen in the streets, where guildhalls and increasingly ...fortable houses appeared.

...own organization and services became more efficient. Drains ...e laid and freshwater springs were channelled towards the city's

public drinking fountains. Arrangements for collecting refuse and rubbish were also made.

Great earthworks banked up and channelled the river. Workshops were set up on the banks and along the irrigation channels; and hydraulic power was harnessed for weaving and paper-making processes.

The port was enlarged and re-organized. An imposing trade hall in the Gothic style was built nearby. The area near the port where the merchants lived and conducted their business grew ever richer, eventually becoming one of the most prestigious districts in Barma. The city was now almost completed, little remaining to be built.

OOPER'S HOUSE
D WORKSHOP

1. **The shop sign**
2. **Well**
3. **Kitchen garden**
4. **Fireplace**
5. **Kitchen**
6. **Shop-cum-workshop**
7. **Attic workshop**
8. **Larder**
9. **Bedrooms**

RAFTSMAN'S HOUSE

...eral different activities went on in the craftsman's house. One ...e rooms was the workshop, where the master craftsman, his

family and his helpers manufactured their special products. The wares were put on sale in the doorway. The upper floors of the house were usually the living quarters of the craftsman's family and their helpers, who might have lodgings there.

Craftsmen's houses backed on to one another, each one supporting the next. They were usually no more than five metres across; this was just enough space for a horse-drawn cart to pull up outside. At the back of the house there was usually a small yard or vegetable patch. A well, either indoors or in the yard, provided water for the household.

From the 13th century onwards, all town houses had chimneys and hearths, which made heating and cooking easier.

Craftsmen's houses were often built on riverbanks or along canals or water channels, as manufacturing processes in the workshop might require quantities of water.

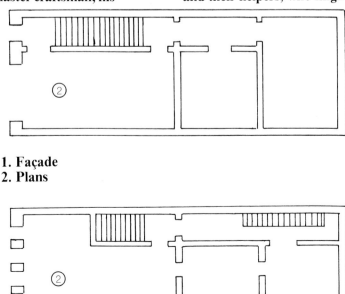

1. **Façade**
2. **Plans**

8. THE RENAISSANCE CITY (early 16th century)

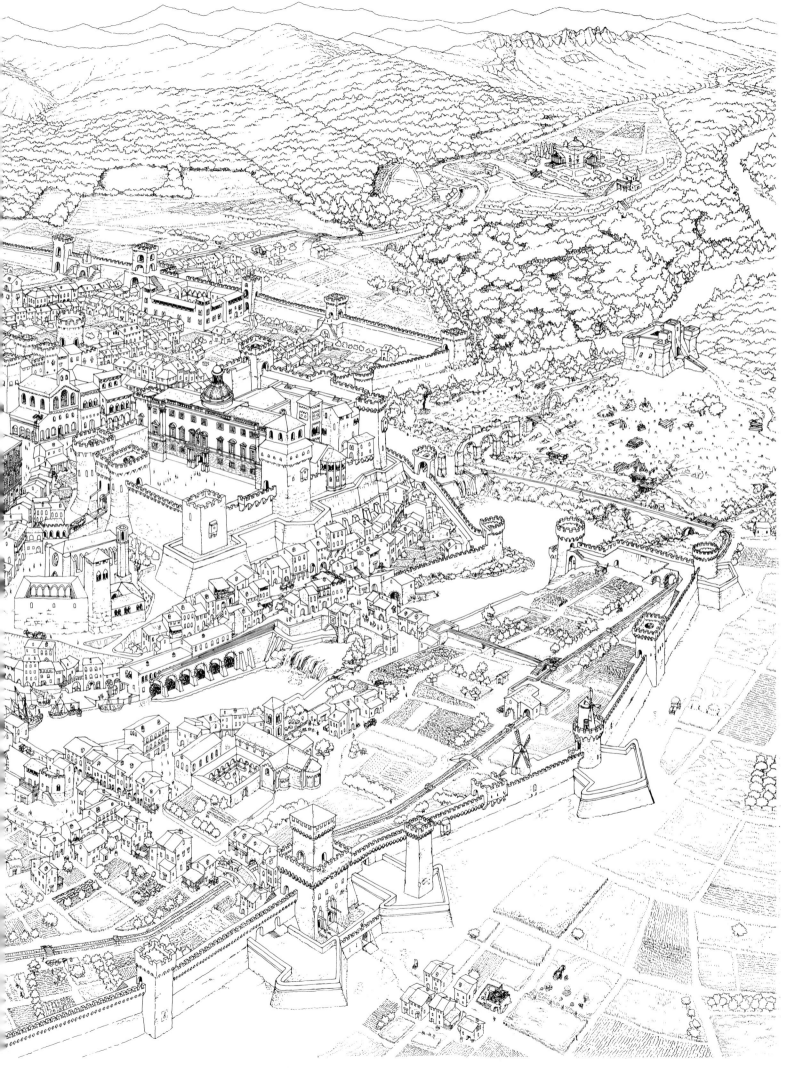

8. THE RENAISSANCE CITY

(EARLY 16TH CENTURY)

By the end of the 15th century, Barma had become a large city. But serious political troubles were affecting the region. Various powerful families were fighting to gain control of the city, and rival European rulers were contending for control of the lower Barmo valley, which each wanted as their territory. These political problems, together with the fall in the population—general in Europe during the Middle Ages—meant that Barma ceased to develop at this time.

In spite of these political difficulties, the city's commercial industrial activities continued to develop. Manufacturing meth improved and new workshops were opened. Merchants prosp from the provisioning of armies, from trade at home and abroad, from banking.

The city that had grown up during the Middle Ages now cease expand and remained within its walls. Work in the city during second half of the 15th century was no longer devoted to enlar the walls but to strengthening them. Soon, engineers, archit

1. Palaces
During the Renaissance, wealthy merchants and a few noblemen became even more powerful. They formed a rich and imperious social class, with power to direct the city's affairs. As symbols of their power, they built themselves large houses and palaces in the fashionable styles of the time.

2. New religious buildings
Architects built impressive churches topped by cupolas. They revived and incorporated some of the features of Greek and Roman temples.

3. Public buildings
Public bodies were kept busy with reorganizing and improving public areas. Public services were improved and streets and squares renovated.

4. The mint
The mint was where money was made. Barma minted its own money, consisting of gold, silver and bronze coins. Inside the mint were moulds, furnaces to melt the precious metal, and other necessary tools.

5. Country houses
Some powerful landowners and noblemen started to modernize and reorganize their estates. They built themselves well-designed, luxurious residences, more like palaces than the farmhouse dwellings they had previously lived in.

A RENAISSANCE CHURCH
1. **Lantern**
2. **Cupola**
3. **Tambour**
4. **Arched vaulting**

ptors, painters and all kinds of craftsmen, each working in the spirit of the Renaissance, transformed Barma into a beautiful dignified city. The city council, the most powerful families, and Church, all rivalled one another in commissioning imposing c, architectural and artistic works. The crowning glory was a e new church dedicated to Saint Eudaldia; its great cupola was ost as spectacular as the one with which Brunelleschi had ned the world a few decades earlier in Florence. The city's streets squares were reorganized and improved, particularly around port. Water splashed out of new public fountains, and fine new ces—built for the ruling families—rose up along the streets,

replacing the old façades.

Because of the frequent battles which had on more than one occasion reached to the very walls of the city, Barma's defences were strengthened. Siege tactics had changed, so that the artillery now needed different methods of defence. The walls were reinforced to make them effective in these altered circumstances.

To protect the part of the city that had grown up on each side of the river, a strong fortress was built on a nearby hill. The old palace, was also strengthened and fortified. During the early 16th century Barma had changed; it had become a modern city.

A RICH MERCHANT FAMILY'S HOUSE

1. **Courtyard**
2. **Well**
3. **Kitchen**
4. **Library**
5. **Loggia**
6. **Bedroom**

9. THE FORTIFIED CITY (mid - 17th century)

9. THE FORTIFIED CITY
(MID - 17TH CENTURY)

In Europe in the 16th and 17th centuries, the great kingdoms formed alliances among themselves. But there were also territorial disputes that led to armed conflict. Barma, since the mid-16th century, had been under the rule of a European king but, because of its strategic importance and economic prosperity, the lower Barmo valley had become disputed territory, over which other powers claimed sovereignty.

Life near the frontier was a nightmare for the inhabitants Barma. They often had to put up with the inconvenience of arm and garrisons sent by the king to defend the city.

The old medieval walls were reinforced in certain places. Basti were built and a wide moat dug. There was a covered walkway i the city and a steep slope ran right the way round below the wa

These new fortifications protected the city against the missile the artillery but they also cut it off from the outside world; for, w the old medieval walls, the width of the fortifications now measu about 100 metres. These walls proved very necessary in the late 1 century and twice during the first half of the 17th century, w

1. Fortified strongholds
The fortifications were re-enforced and strengthened to protect the city's weak points. These extra ramparts housed the artillery. They were very strong and difficult to breach.

2. Baroque gateway
As in previous periods, gateways were few. Now, however, they were defended by extra fortifications. This gateway is in the Baroque style, characteristic of 17th century military architecture.

3. Bastions
The bastion was a basic feature of modern ramparts. It housed the bulk of the artillery and was the defensive position from which attackers were repelled. Each bastion was carefully positioned so that firepower could be effectively combined.

4. The moat
Attackers were forced to approach the city by crossing the wide defensive moat in full view of the defenders. The moat was situated between the walls and the outer side of the ditch, which with the inside slope, formed the first line of defence.

5. The ruler's palace
The old palace was turned into the ruler's residence, overlooking the armed garrison. The whole fortification became a small stronghold inside the city.

6. The Baroque church
Some palaces and religious buildings were built or altered in t Baroque style, characteristic the 17th century.

ARTILLERY AND FORTIFICATIONS
By the 16th century, artillery had became much more effective that the old medieval walls (1) were easily destroyed by cannonf (2). During the 17th and 18th centuries many medieval walls w reinforced or rebuilt. Deep moats (3) were dug and parapets (4) a bastions (5) were added. A wide slope called a berm (6) protected wall against the impact of the enemy's artillery. With these n fortifications, besieging a fortress became a long and diffic business.

10. ENLIGHTENMENT AND INDUSTRY
(MID - 18TH CENTURY)

In the mid-18th century, major changes took place in the way trade and industry worked in Barma. Successful merchants agreed among themselves not to pay the high prices which the guilds were demanding for their goods. Instead, they decided to run their own factories and workshops and to bring in poorly-paid peasants from the countryside to work in them. Factories made their fi[rst] appearance; they were strange-looking places and, unlike a cra[fts]man's workshop, which was also his house, production of goods w[as] the only thing that went on there.

The factory owner brought workmen and labourers into [the] factory and made them work in return for a wage. Altho[ugh] production processes remained basically the same, organization a[nd] the division of labour resulted in lower prices than those deman[ded] by the craftsmen. This resulted in a bitter struggle between [the] craftsmen and the factory owners but the craftsmen's guilds w[ere] eventually defeated.

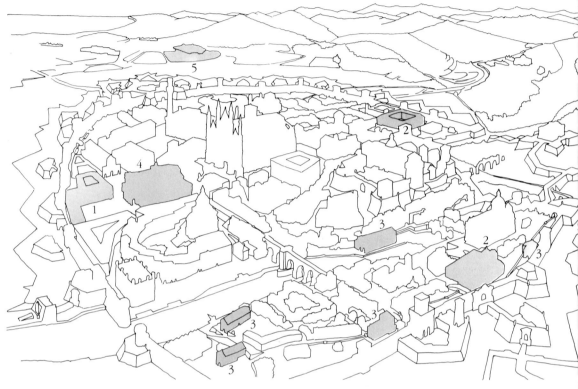

1. The Chamber of Commerce
Merchants and businessmen formed organizations to promote economic development. One of these was the Chamber of Commerce; it gave businessmen information and provided various services. In keeping with the spirit of the Age of Enlightenment, businessmen arranged educational courses for themselves, and set up scientific experiments. The classes emphasized practical matters, however, in contrast to the old university, which still taught the traditional subjects of the Middle Ages.

2. Military headquarters
The Age of Enlightenment saw the appearance of the first military headquarters, which were to house the weapons of the king's standing army. Before these were built, private households were forced to take in soldiers, at great inconvenience to themselves.

3. The factories
Apart from a few examples built in the neo-Classical style, facto-ries were not very impressive buildings. Inside, workers toiled in crowded conditions, busy with the manufacture of goods. Some factories used hydraulic power to turn wheels and gears to speed up the production processes.

4. The opera house
The theatre and, especially, the opera reached a peak of popularity at the time. Performances were given in specially-designed buildings. The opera house soon became one of the city's most prestigious buildings.

5. Quarantine camps
These were set up outside t[he] city walls to house people wi[th] infectious diseases. The cam[ps] were burned once the epidem[ic] was over.

A PAPER MILL
Water-driven machinery that worked the various mechanical devices used in paper-making.

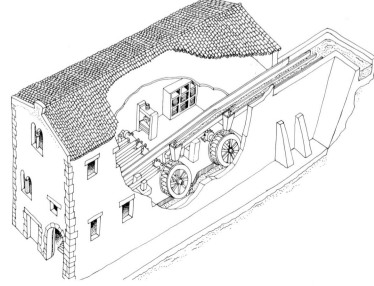

PAPER-MAKING
The first great factories for t[he] production of textiles, cerami[cs] and paper appeared in the 18[th] century. The use of hydrau[lic] power in production process[es] was a major technical impro[ve]ment.
1. **Rags**
2. **Mechanical beaters reduci[ng] rags to pulp**
3. **Making sheets of paper**
4. **Pressing**
5. **Drying**
6. **Smoothing machine**

he government strongly supported the factory owners and they n shook off restrictions imposed by the guilds, and were free to anize production methods exactly as they pleased.

actories changed the face of the urban landscape. At first, they e large buildings of two or more storeys, standing starkly out n their surroundings. As more and more were built, workers noured to work in them. Peasants and immigrants trekked to the in search of work. As for the craftsmen, many of those who had n ruined by competition became factory workers. Many crafts-n's houses were turned into living quarters for the workers' ilies; sometimes an extra floor or two was added on above.

Under the government of a king who ruled in the tradition of enlightened despotism, Barma now enjoyed a period of peace. At the beginning of the 18th century, the city and entire surrounding area had risen up in revolt, but after fierce battles the rebellion was put down by government troops. The king punished Barma by taking away the city's privilege of self-government and placing it under the control of a military commander. Fortifications were strengthened and headquarters were built to prevent any further uprisings.

The king encouraged manufacture and commerce, and set his military engineers to work on projects such as road-building.

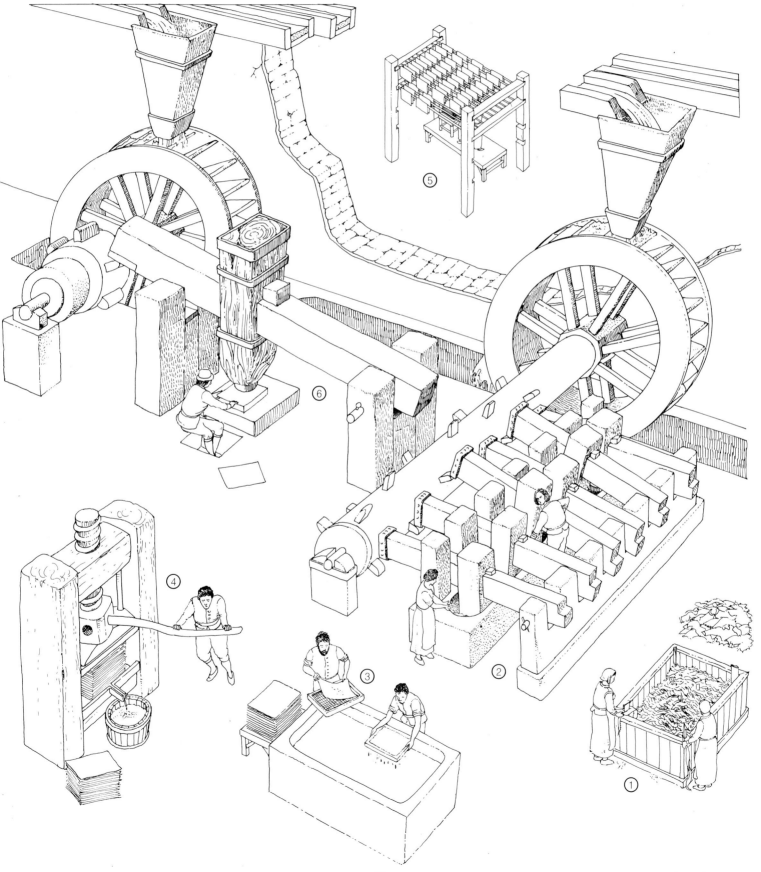

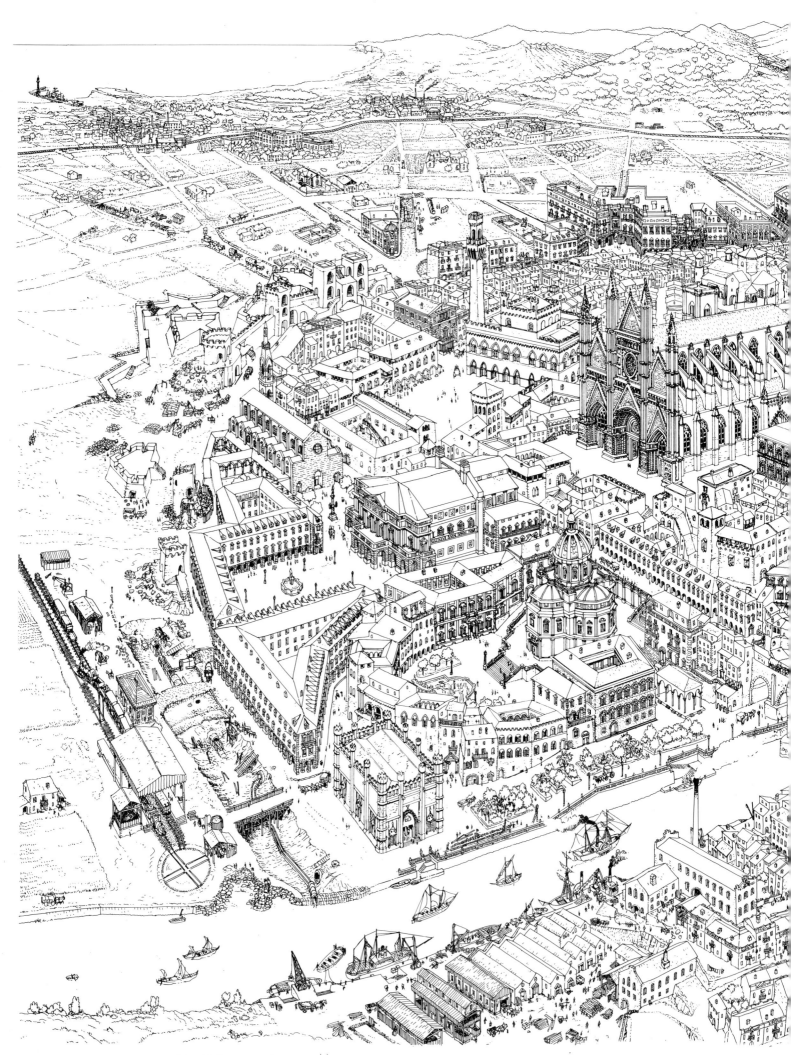

11. THE STEAM AGE (mid - 19th century)

11. THE STEAM AGE
(MID - 19TH CENTURY)

Barma adjusted slowly to technological change and advances in manufacturing techniques. In the 1830s, an industrialist decided to install a steam-driven machine in his factory. This solved the energy problem and brought about the introduction of machinery that was already in use in factories all over northern Europe.

The arrival of the first steam-driven machines marked the beginning of a frantic race for mechanization. Although Barma was only a medium-sized city, with a manufacturing tradition, chimneys soon sprang up along its skyline, rivalling the old chimney towers. New factories appeared in the heart of the city alterations were carried out to the docks so that they could ha the loading and unloading of coal.

Hundreds of people arrived from the countryside to look work, eventually settling in the city. More storeys were added the old craftsmen's houses, to accommodate the new populat and many new buildings were built to house the workers. Sho before the middle of the century, the city's population had reac about 40,000.

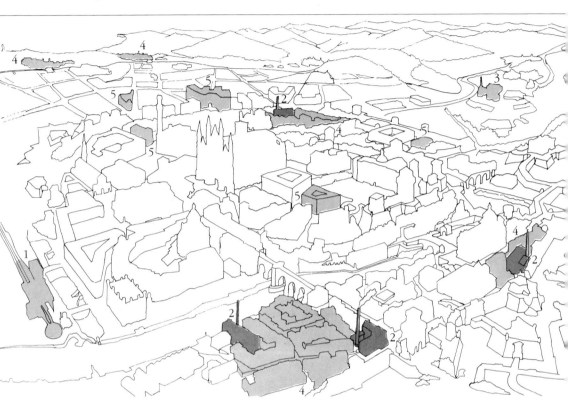

1. The railway station
The railway changed the face of the urban landscape. Symbolizing progress, it was one of the driving forces behind 19th-century industrialization. Steam engines capable of travelling at a terrifying 50 kph made travel and transport easier.

2. Steam mills
These were built in the industrialized areas of Southern Europe from about 1830. They had tall chimneys and workshops were arranged each side of long aisles. Most of them were built like British factories and were equipped with British machinery.

3. The gasworks
Gas became an important element in 19th-century city life. Streets and public buildings, as well as private houses, were lit by gas. The gas was channelled in wide underground pipes to various points where it was needed.

4. Workers' ghettoes
Many of the old districts of the city where craftsmen had once worked were taken over by the working classes. Overpopulation and squalor soon followed. In some parts of the city where there was still room to build, *housing for the middle and working classes was provided. These dwellings were all built to the same design.*

5. New buildings
The mid-19th century city saw the first appearance of various *public buildings. These inclu banks, a number of priv schools, a main post office the fire station.*

HOW A CRAFTSMAN'S HOUSE EVOLVED

As time went by, the old craftsmen's areas in some parts of the city were taken over by the working classes. Having lost their original purpose, craftspeople's dwellings were converted into flats. One or more working-class families lived in each of these. These houses grew upwards. People went in through a small door at the front and climbed a flight of stairs leading to all the floors.

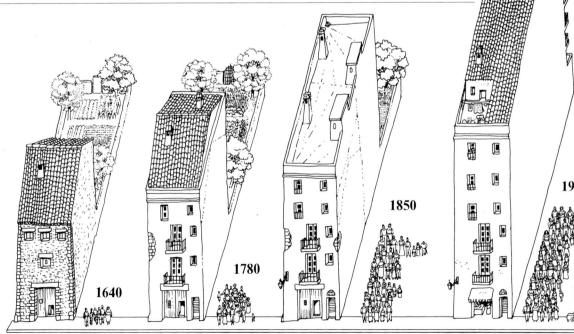

1640   1780   1850   19

he inner city had reached saturation point. There was now no
e room to build new factories or accommodation for the
kers, or houses for the middle classes.

he walls that had protected the city for so long were now a noose
was threatening to strangle it. Even so, the military authorities
convinced that the walls were strategically important for the
and necessary for controlling its rebellious population, and they
ade their demolition.

espite the overcrowded conditions inside the city walls, municipal
ices improved greatly. Every house had main drains and the
nage system was improved generally. Gasworks were installed

for the provision of street lighting. The city council also introduced
new services, such as refuse collections and fire brigades. New
buildings, including public institutions such as banks and post
offices, jostled for space in the crowded centre.

During the 1840s Barma was to accommodate something completely new; this was the railway line, which linked the city with the
lower Barmo valley.

In the mid-19th century, the government gave permission for the
walls to be knocked down. Within a few years, the whole system of
ramparts had been dismantled. At the same time, planning and
building of suburbs began in open ground around the city.

/ORKING-CLASS
RTMENT HOUSE

nes for the workers and
families were built close to
actories or on new industrial
tes.

lat
edrooms
itchen
avatory
ell
esspit

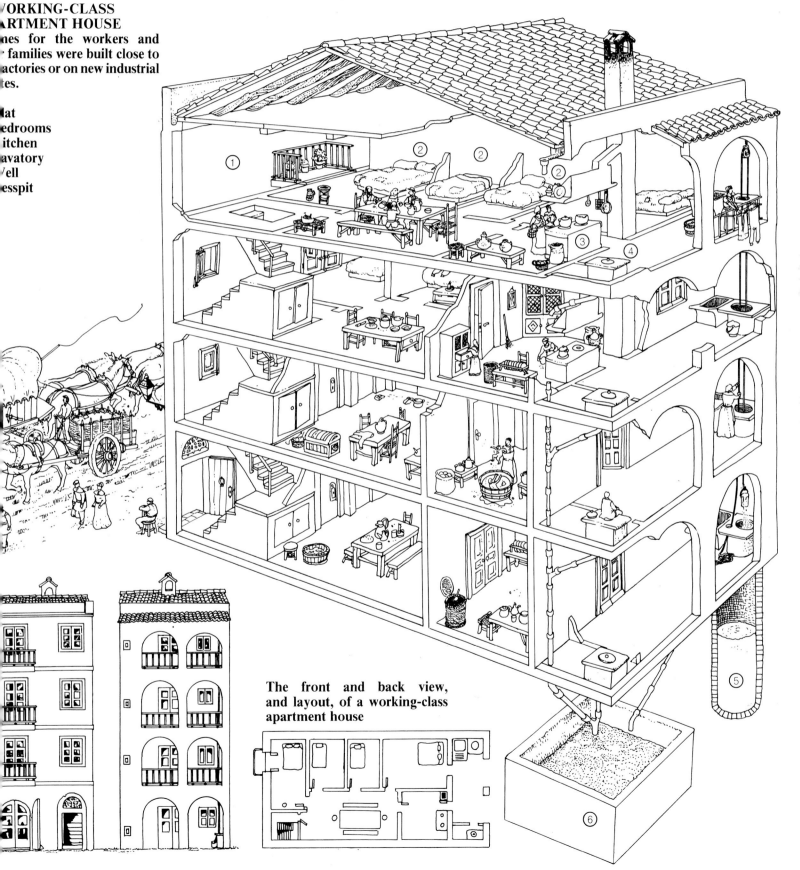

The front and back view,
and layout, of a working-class
apartment house

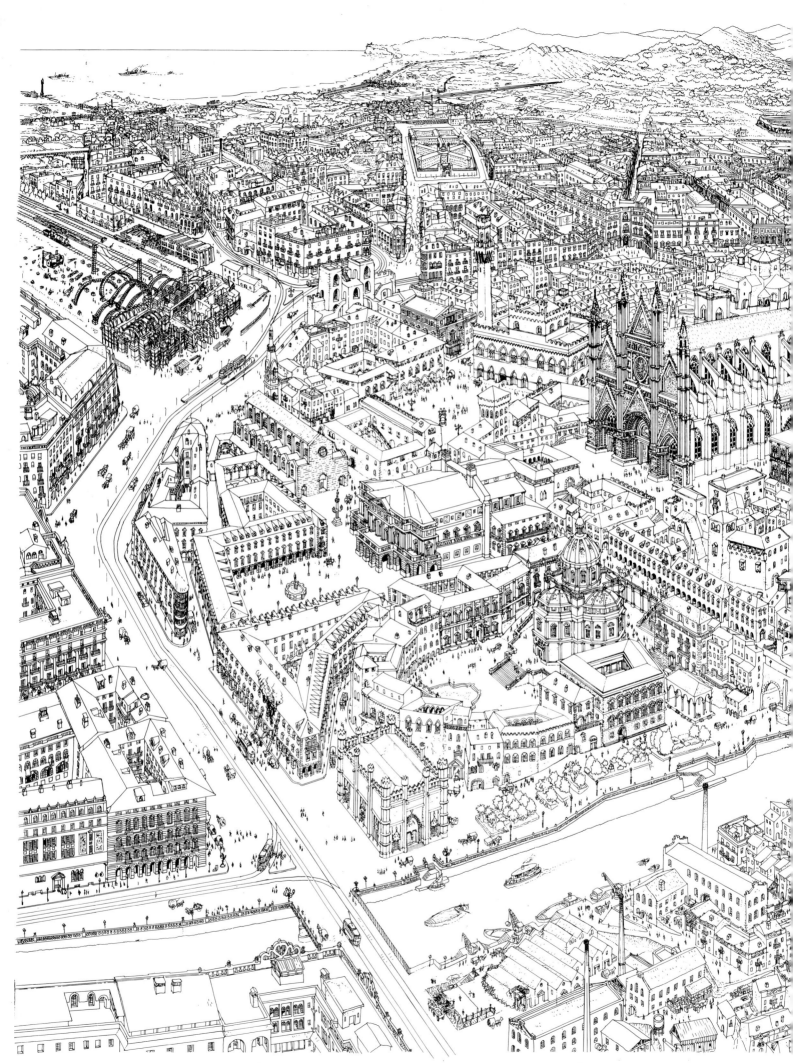

12. SUBURBAN EXPANSION (early 20th century)

51

12. SUBURBAN EXPANSION
(EARLY 20TH CENTURY)

Barma's expansion during the second half of the 19th century had been spectacular. After the walls had been knocked down, the ground they had stood on was turned into wide avenues that encircled the city.

Now, building in the areas outside the walls began. The council's efforts to direct this expansion were largely unsuccessfu private speculators and contractors took the project into their hands.

Houses set in spacious residential areas were soon built fo middle classes, and for the upper classes who commissi luxurious residences and even small palaces. Other areas reserved for industry, with factories and working-class suburb:

By the beginning of the 20th century, Barma's population reached about 100,000, including the outer industrial areas w were also part of the city. The appearance of the city had alt

1. The power station
Increasing demand for electricity in industry and for transport and municipal services led to the installation of a power station. Large quantities of coal were burnt in it to produce electricity.

2. The market
Large markets were built where people could buy food and everyday provisions from all kinds of stalls. Some markets were impressive structures, often built with metal arches and roofed with glass.

3. The hospital
The city's expansion and the improvement of municipal services led to the establishment of new and modern hospitals. The old medieval institutions were no longer adequate for modern standards of hygiene and could not cope effectively with the demands of the day.

4. The football ground
Sporting facilities were provided in response to the growing popularity of spectator sports and sport in general. Football, as a popular sport, began to spread at the end of the 19th century.

5. New buildings
As the city developed, a number of buildings appeared which had so far not been important features of the townscape. These included newspaper offices, a modern prison, which had

replaced the old medieval d geons, tram depots, cinemas telephone exchange, a telegr office and new bank branch

SANITATION
Newly built houses were equipped with modern sanitation. Lavatories and bath tubs, with hot and cold water, were the great innovations of the age.

...iderably, not only because of the growth of the suburbs but also ...use of modernization. The use of electricity brought a range of ...rovements; many factories now used this new form of energy, ...street lighting and transport were gradually converted. The tram ...the urban transport system of the age and tramlines, tram stops ...trams themselves, all became features of the new city.

... power station was built to provide electricity. New buildings ...e built for modern lifestyles; there were tram depots, a new ...way station, food markets, state schools, libraries and museums. ...icularly noticeable because of their size and imposing appearance ...e the new university, the hospital, the central fruit and vegetable market, the slaughterhouse, the prison and the cemetery.

New building technology using iron and concrete, together with the spread of new styles such as Art Nouveau and Modernism, gave rise to impressive architectural structures and bold designs.

The administration of Barma improved greatly; the city authorities made sure that every house in the outer suburbs had drinking water and main drainage, and these facilities were also modernized in the old city centre.

INNER CITY STREET

block of flats for the urban middle class
ewer
as mains
Water mains
lectricity supply post
ram
obbled street
as lamp

13. THE MODERN CITY (mid - 20th century)

13. THE MODERN CITY
(MID - 20TH CENTURY)

During the first half of the 20th century, Barma continued to undergo considerable expansion and change. Its population grew enormously so that, by the mid-century, the total number of inhabitants, including those in the suburbs and outlying districts, had reached about 250,000.

Areas further and further away from the city centre became built up. Meanwhile the centre itself and existing suburbs were constantly changing. As a result of serious bomb damage during the Sec[ond] World War (1939-45), whole streets of buildings had been lef[t in] ruins. Now these were rebuilt. However, the most important fa[ctor] in the city at this time was land speculation. Land prices in cen[tral] areas, alongside main roads, and in shopping and administra[tive] centres, rose sharply. Many houses were sold and knocked dow[n to] make room for spectacular new buildings. Factories gradu[ally] moved to the outskirts of the city, and the plots of land on which t[hey] stood were sold for development at inflated prices.

Different architectural styles and fashions came and went in ra[pid] succession throughout the century. Modernism and eclectic[ism]

1. Centres of trade and administration
Some areas of the city became centres of trade and administration; others contained blocks of commercial offices. The impressively tall buildings of large companies stood out on the skyline.

2. Parks and open spaces
The quality of life in the city was improved by the preservation of grassy areas where people could relax.

3. Luxury residences
Luxurious residences were built in certain areas, for the wealthiest and most privileged people.

4. The housing estate
Industrial workers, immigrants and people with low incomes lived in large housing estates which were not always well maintained. These were built on the outskirts or sometimes in old derelict areas of the city.

5. The industrial estate
Industrial areas were built further and further away from the city centre as the search for cheaper land and more space continued. By contrast with the 19th-century worker, who had been able to walk to work, the 20th-century worker had to t[ra]vel great distances from the c[ity] outskirts or housing estate.

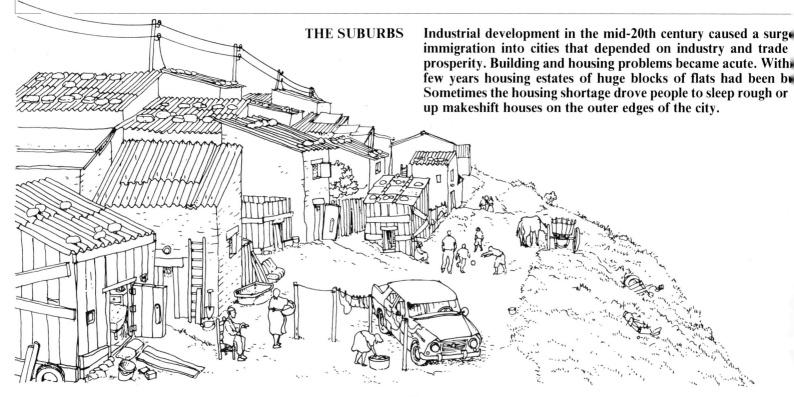

THE SUBURBS

Industrial development in the mid-20th century caused a surg[e in] immigration into cities that depended on industry and trade [for] prosperity. Building and housing problems became acute. With[in a] few years housing estates of huge blocks of flats had been b[uilt]. Sometimes the housing shortage drove people to sleep rough or [put] up makeshift houses on the outer edges of the city.

peted with more traditional approaches to building. These, in
, were at odds with the monumental architectural style favoured
lictators during their periods of power in the early 20th century.
rom the 1930s, Barma had its first skyscrapers, but these were
shadows of their North American counterparts. After the war,
tendency for many buildings to be constructed vertically
ained.

he post-war years and the great economic revival that followed
affected Barma. The heart of the old city and the inner suburbs,
ch now made up the city centre, became the centre of commerce,
a large number of shops and offices, and business head-

quarters. While this frenzied building activity was taking place in the
city centre, industrial estates were being built on the outskirts of the
city. Huge housing estates for the new working class were also built
as the result of post-war industrial expansion.

Many streets were metalled and the car was becoming a popular
means of transport for those who could afford it.

Water and electricity supplies and a main drainage system were
common throughout the city. Underground and over-ground railway
lines were also constructed.

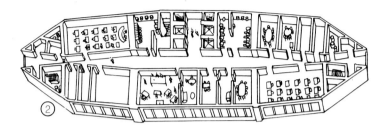

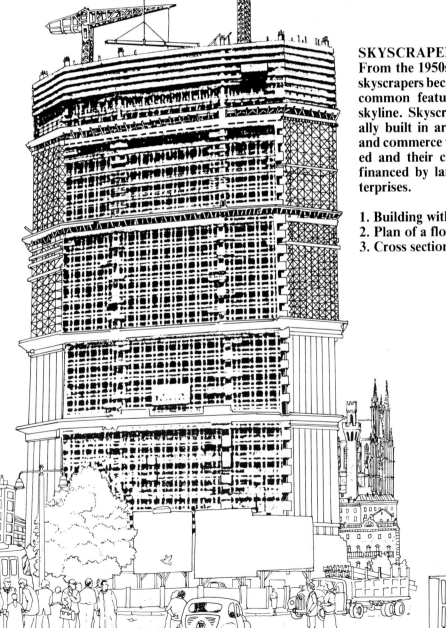

SKYSCRAPERS
From the 1950s onwards, huge
skyscrapers became increasingly
common features on the city
skyline. Skyscrapers were usually built in areas where trade
and commerce were concentrat-
ed and their construction was
financed by large business en-
terprises.

1. Building with steel girders
2. Plan of a floor of offices
3. Cross section of a skyscraper

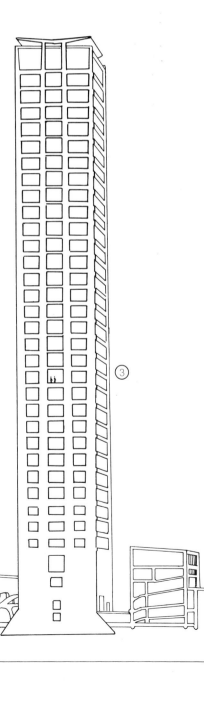

14. LOOKING TO THE FUTURE (the late 20th century)

14. LOOKING TO THE FUTURE
(THE LATE 20TH CENTURY)

By the late 20th century, the population of Barma had increased enormously and the whole metropolitan area now supported about 350,000 inhabitants. This growth was mostly due to industrial expansion following the Second World War. From the 1980s onwards, however, population growth slowed down and, in some areas, tended to decrease. The city centre became even more stro[n] geared towards commerce and administration and smaller busi[ness] centres were built on the outskirts.

Some industries based in the outskirts were moved even fur[ther] out and the space they had taken up was given over to housin[g] turned into parks or public gardens.

Almost everyone owned a car. Cars and lorries on the ro[ads] traffic lights and public car parks, among other things, dramatic[ally] altered the appearance of the city and the daily life of the citize[ns.] Tramways disappeared with the rapid increase of car own[ership.] Driving in or out of the city became extremely difficult. An atte[mpt]

1. Freeways and ring roads
The increase in traffic and over-crowding on the roads made it very difficult to enter and leave the city. An attempt to solve the problem was made by building ring roads and freeways.

2. Natural parkland
The hills that in ancient times had been far away from the city centre now seemed very near. These were turned into parkland, providing an essential breathing space within easy reach of the city.

3. Converted buildings
Some of the buildings that had lost their original purpose were used by other business ventures, or were converted into cultural or entertainment centres.

4. Arts and sports centres
The fact that people had more spare time encouraged participation in sport, the arts and spectator sports. Buildings and open spaces were converted for these activities and leisure centres were constructed.

5. The telecommunications tower
The widespread use of televisions, radios, telephones and telecommunications made it necessary to build a high tow[er] for receiving and transmitt[ing] signals. With its characteris[tic] profile, the tower quickly [be]came part of the city skyline.

A BLOCK OF FLATS
1. Lift
2. Underground car park

A STREET
3. Street lighting
4. Telephone box
5. Traffic lights

BENEATH THE STREET
  6. Sewer
  7. Water main
  8. Drain
  9. Gas main
10. Telephone cables
11. Electricity cables

UNDERGROUND RAILWAY
12. Entrance
13. Station
14. Tunnels

olve the problem was made by building ring roads and slip roads
ing onto motorways and freeways but traffic still moved slowly.
ramped conditions, air and noise pollution, and other problems
ted to life in a large city, all contributed to the transformation of
ma into an unattractive and inhuman place in which to live.
arma had grown too large. It was difficult to administer and its
abitants produced great quantities of refuse and all kinds of litter
destroyed the distinctive quality of the city.

Determined to stop this process of deterioration, the municipal
orities started to control expansion. They stopped the destruction
he city's historical and artistic heritage, limited the amount of
new building work in certain areas and preserved the most
interesting buildings. They introduced a policy of restoration and
efforts were made to avoid further damage to the city's ancient centre
and surrounding areas. Many buildings, including fine old palaces
and early factories, were restored and opened to the public. The
creation of more parks and open spaces resulted in more sports
grounds. These in turn produced greater traffic pollution and the
need for more traffic control.

The city needs to overcome the problems created by overpopulation
in the second half of the 20th century; to restore the quality of life
and to make the city, once more, a pleasant place in which to live.

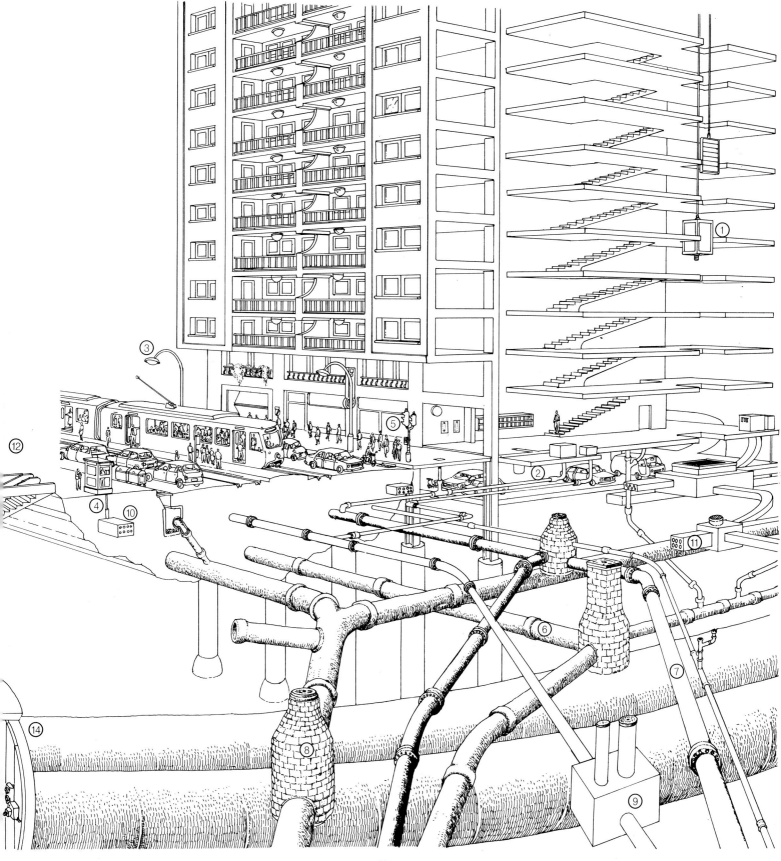

GLOSSARY

Age of Enlightenment An 18th-century philosophical movement.

Allegiance Loyalty.

Amphitheatre An open circular or oval building with tiers of seats rising from a central arena.

Barbarians Brutal and uncivilized people, especially those living outside the Roman Empire.

Basilica A Roman building used for public administration. Later, an early Christian church.

Brunelleschi An Italian architect (1377-1446) who built the dome of the cathedral at Florence and other great buildings.

Buttress A stone construction built to support a wall.

Chamber of Commerce A group of townspeople who oversee the running of commerce in a town or city.

Classical Relating to or characteristic of the civilization of the Ancient Greeks and Romans.

Cloister Covered walks around a quadrangle, usually in a religious building.

Cupola A small domed structure on top of a roof or dome.

Eclecticism Selecting what seems best from various styles, ideas, methods etc.

Enlightened despotism The rule of a benevolent tyrant.

Entrepreneur The owner of a business enterprise who, by taking risks and initiative, attempts to make profits.

Feudal system The legal and social system that evolved in Western Europe in the 8th and 9th centuries.

Forum A public meeting place in Ancient Rome.

Ghetto A densely populated slum area of a city.

Glaziers People who fit glass into windows.

Guilds Associations of men formed in medieval Europe to g mutual aid and protection and to maintain craft standards.

Hannibal A Carthaginian general who invaded Italy with his tro in the Second Punic War (218-201 BC).

Heretics People holding beliefs contrary to the established teachi of the Church.

Hydraulic power Power produced by the pressure of water.

Legion A military unit of the Roman army, made up of infantry v supporting cavalry, numbering between 3,000 and 6,000 me

Loggia A porch or covered area on the side of a building.

Metropolitan Relating to the main city or capital.

Municipal Relating to the local government of a town or city.

Nave The central space in a church.

Nomadic Describing people who move from place to pla originally in search of pasture and food.

Portico A covered entrance to a building.

Ramparts Fortified walls built for defence.

Rhetoric The study of the technique of using language to persu and influence people.

Rotating crops Growing different crops in succession on the sa land, so that the soil can regain fertility.

Speculators People who buy and sell at high risk, hoping to m high profits.

Tambour A circular wall supporting a dome or one that surrounded by a colonnade.

Theology The study of the teaching of the Christian Church.

FURTHER READING

Bolwell, Laurie and Lines, Cliff *How Towns Grow and Change* (Wayland, 1985)

Hope, Robert *Cities* (Macdonald, 1984)

Macaulay, David *Cathedral, The story of its construction* (Collins, 1974)

Macaulay, David *City, A story of Roman planning and construction* (Collins, 1975)

Neal, Philip *The Urban Scene* (Dryad Press, 1987)

Van Zandt, Eleanor *Architecture* (Wayland, 1989)

of Enlightenment 44
culture 8-9
…hitheatre 16
…tment house 49
…educt 16
…ustus, Emperor 16
…ues 52

…ks and banking 32, 36, 48
…arians 20, 21
…ica 16, 21
…s 12, 16
…les 8, 12, 20, 21, 29, 36, 40
…b damage 56
…ge building 12-13, 20
…nelleschi 37
…antines 21

…ls 28
…57, 60-61
…thage 12
…edral 24-5, 28-29
…mber of Commerce 44
…rlemagne, Emperor 24
…istianity, arrival of 20-21
…istians 20, 21
…walls 14, 20, 24, 28, 32, 36, 40-41, 49
…stantine, Emperor 20
…vents 32
…smen 25, 28, 29, 44
…s 8-9, 16

…nage system 12, 17, 33, 53
…king water 16, 33, 36

…dom 24
…tricity 53

…ories 44-5, 48-9, 52, 56
…ning 8-9, 17, 24
…alism 24
…49, 57, 61
…ball ground 52
…ifications 8, 13, 20, 37, 40-41, 45
…m 16

gasworks 48
Greeks 8
guilds 28, 33, 45

Hannibal 12
Holy Roman Empire 41
hospital 29, 52
houses 8, 9, 16-17, 25, 28, 29, 33, 37, 48, 49,
    52, 53
housing estate 53, 56, 57
housing shortage 48, 57
hydraulic power 33

immigrants 36, 45, 56
industrial estates 48, 56
industrial expansion 48-9, 57, 60
insulae 17
iron-working 9
irrigation 25, 33

Jewish people 29
Jewish quarter 25

land speculation 56

markets 32, 52, 53
merchants 28, 32, 36, 38, 44
mint 37
monasteries 24-5, 32
monastic buildings 28, 33

nomadic peoples 8

olive groves 8
opera house 44
overpopulation 48, 61

palaces 20, 24, 28, 36, 40
paper-making 41, 44-5
parks 56, 60
plague 32
pollution 60-61
population growth 17, 25, 28, 32, 36, 41, 48,
    56, 60
power station 52
public buildings 17, 49, 52-3

railway 49, 57
ramparts 8, 20
rebellion 20
Renaissance 36
ring roads 60-61
river port 17, 28, 33, 41, 48
road building 12-13, 44
Roman camp 12-13
Roman Empire 12-13, 16
    decline of 20-21
Roman legion 12, 16

sanitation 53
schools 52
settlements 12
shops 16, 17, 33
shrines 20-21
siege 40-41
skyscrapers 56, 57
slaves 13, 16
sports centres 60
steam mills 48
storage pits 8
street lighting 52
suburbs 52, 56, 57

telecommunications tower 60
telephone exchange 52
theatre 16, 44
tower houses 28, 33
town council 28
town hall 28, 32
town planners 12
trade 8, 12, 13, 16, 25, 28, 33, 56
traffic 60
Trajan, Emperor 16
trams 53

underground railway 57, 60
university 24, 28, 29, 32, 44, 52

vineyards 8

warriors 8, 21
water mills 24, 25
woollen cloth 28, 41
workshops 16, 17, 28, 32, 44